LifeVesting

Praise for *LiveVesting*

Imagine having a conversation with an intimate friend - someone who reminds you that despite your failures, you are not defined by your past, and you are the author of ANY future you wish to create. That's what it's like to read *LifeVesting*, and as Andy says, let *LifeVesting* read you! This book will show you the indescribable JOY of living in the freedom and abundance made possible through God's grace to every believer. Your future and eternity are calling – *LifeVesting* can show you the way.

Shannon Ethridge, M.A.

Coach, Mentor, and

Author of 22 books, including the

million-copy, best-selling *Every Woman's Battle* series

Get ready to hear the song of your heart. *LifeVesting* is a call to every believer, with the Spirit as your guide, to listen, hear and respond to the unique lifesong God has given you. Whether that sends you around the world or simply across the room, Andy Wood has provided a 'coach approach' to living full-out. Grab your journaling pen, find your quiet place, and listen for the song God wrote just for you!

Christopher McCluskey, PCC

President, Professional Christian Coaching Institute

Andy Wood has given you a pathway to taking ownership of your future and finding the fulfillment of your most cherished dreams. Here you will find the encouragement, wisdom, and practical tools you need finish strong. *LifeVesting* is personal, practical, biblical, and challenging. A great resource for entrepreneurs, leaders, coaches, and anyone who's determined to make their lives count.

Kim Avery

Co-host of the *Professional Christian Coaching Today* Podcast,

Author of *The Prayer Powered Entrepreneur*

How do we live a life, so the use of our life, outlives our life? A legacy is what we leave in other people during our time here. I love how the author shares exactly how to create a life that gives more than it takes and energizes more than it exhausts. The framework of *LifeVesting* is so practical and actionable. This is a book every Kingdom driven entrepreneur and business person should read and apply. Thank you for writing this!

John Ramstead
CEO Beyond Influence,
Author of *On Purpose With Purpose*
Executive Coach and Leadership Expert

In *LifeVesting*, Andy Wood declares that you only have one life and an endless array of choices for how to invest it. He then provides a practical guidebook to navigate these choices to help you get the most out of life while positively impacting others for the Kingdom of God. This book is a must-read for anyone who wants to invest his or her life in a way that produces a fruitful abundance.

Jon Lokhorst
Author of *Mission-Critical Leadership:*
How Smart Managers Lead Well in All Directions

LifeVesting is life transformational gold! Andy Wood takes the universal and practical truths of life and makes them simple and helpful so that every person can apply them to life and be successful. The book is totally holistic in its approach addressing the mind, body, soul, and spirit of an individual and how they can make a long-term impact in the future through the lifestyle choices you make today and the life map you follow. It was a joy to read and practical to follow with simple insights into the soul and encouragement to lifevest into the future. A must read for all those seeking direction.

Andrew Oates
Executive Pastor, Coastal Community Church
Yorktown, VA

In order to finish well, we need to live well. Andy Wood's book *LifeVesting: Cultivate a Life of Abundance, Impact, and Freedom* is filled with the tools and strategies you need to make a positive difference in your life and in the lives of others. If you want to make wise choices and live intentionally, begin today with this wonderful life-changing book.

Georgia Shaffer
Professional Certified Coach
PA Licensed Psychologist
Author of *Coaching the Coach: Life Coaching Stories and Tips for Transforming Lives.*

"It is never too late to start investing." Those words are not only true in retirement, but in every area of life. The book, *LifeVesting* by Andy Wood gives us the right tools to make an impact. An impact in eternity. An impact in our family. An impact for our legacy. Although the book is written in simple terms, there are deep, complex principles given. Easy to read and easy to apply. Thank you, Andy for developing a path for those of us who want to have a monumental return on our daily investment of our life."

Scott Dawson
Scott Dawson Evangelistic Association
twitter @scottdawson

Andy Wood has a real gift of taking powerful, sometimes hard to understand, biblical truths and making them understandable and applicable. LIFEVESTING mirrors his coaching/mentoring style; organized impactful content sprinkled with humor and personal stories. That's a great recipe for those desiring a paradigm shift from success to significance…from living to ABUNDANT living!

Alan Floyd
Lead Pastor of Cottage Hill Church
Mobile, AL

Reading Andy's book is like getting leadership advice from a seasoned expert, all while casually enjoying a glass of iced tea with him! His book reads so seamlessly that at the end of each chapter, you'll be amazed at the ground you've covered together. Andy takes big leadership concepts and makes them approachable, practical, and immediately applicable. Lifevesting is a must read for anyone in leadership ready for a down-to-earth approach to growing your mind, body, spirit, and love.

Kyle Bullock
Writer, Podcaster, Entrepreneur at KyleRBullock.com

Dr. Wood is a gifted university professor who blesses students with a quality learning environment. This book is a great way for his content to be available to anyone. The same engaging style he uses to teach students is also found in this book. You will experience excellent concepts related to leadership and life and be able to apply them in practical ways. I enjoyed this book very much.

Kathy Crockett, Ph.D.
Executive Coach,
Founder of Crockett+Co - Professional Development

LifeVesting

Cultivate a Life
of Abundance, Impact
and Freedom

ANDY WOOD

MOUNT
TABOR
MEDIA

NASHVILLE

NEW YORK • LONDON • MELBOURNE • VANCOUVER

LifeVesting

Cultivate a Life of Abundance, Impact and Freedom

Published in New York, New York, by Mount Tabor Media, a branded imprint of Morgan James Publishing. Morgan James is a trademark of Morgan James, LLC. www.MorganJamesPublishing.com

Proudly distributed by Ingram Publisher Services.

Morgan James BOGO™

A **FREE** ebook edition is available for you or a friend with the purchase of this print book.

CLEARLY SIGN YOUR NAME ABOVE

Instructions to claim your free ebook edition:
1. Visit MorganJamesBOGO.com
2. Sign your name CLEARLY in the space above
3. Complete the form and submit a photo of this entire page
4. You or your friend can download the ebook to your preferred device

ISBN 9781631956058 paperback
ISBN 9781631956065 ebook
Library of Congress Control Number:
2021936438

Cover & Interior Design by:
Christopher Kirk
www.GFSstudio.com

MOUNT TABOR MEDIA
VERITUM REVELATUM - "TRUTH REVEALED"
A BRANDED IMPRINT OF MORGAN JAMES

Dedication

To Joel, my "face in the window,"
who started all this with a simple, elegant idea . . .
then mercilessly harassed me, encouraged me, and cheered me on until it was done.

Table of Contents

Acknowledgments

E very lasting structure has a strong foundation, and that's where I begin. This year has been a bittersweet reminder of the three men who, in addition to my parents, greatly influenced my life and leadership. While Rick Cagle passed away several years ago, his influence ("Tell you what you need to do...") lives on in me and all who knew him. The other two – my pastor Fred Wolfe and his long-time worship leader Ed Keyes – both entered into their eternal reward earlier this year. I miss all three of these men greatly, but their spiritual DNA still courses through my heart. And you could trace their influence in the pages of this book if you knew where to look.

Special thanks to my wife, Robin, for her 38-years-and-counting investment in my life and work. For all the times you listened patiently as I read different parts of this material to you (or let me serenade you to sleep with it), thank you. For the times when you reflected the vision of "the brand" faithfully and boldly in places ranging from Texas to Thailand, thank you.

To my three adult children, Carrie, Cassie, and Joel, who now with their amazing spouses are investing in future generations of their own, who inspired the original idea and cheered it on, thank you.

Special thanks to my friend Christopher McCluskey, who invested in me as a coach and convinced me that I could build a Kingdom-loving, financially sound business by taking these principles and investing them in leaders, business owners, entrepreneurs, and anyone with a dream – then made a way to have this book published. That conversation around the fire pit in the rolling hills of Missouri set the wheels in motion. Words are inadequate to express my sense of honor and gratitude.

To the coaches who have invested in me through the last several years – Kim Avery, John Ramstead, and Michael Pfau – a special thank-you for your wisdom, encouragement, and transformative work. May you receive in return even more than you have blessed me.

My editor, the brilliant Janis Whipple, worked magic with the manuscript, and the team at Morgan James Publishing have been nothing short of encouraging and professional, starting with the delightful (and patient!) Gayle West.

Four years ago my friend and pastor Alan Floyd came to see me in the hospital when a health scare brought me to a major life crossroads. "Don't forget LifeVesting," he said. And our regular LifeVesting dream sessions have been a major motivator over the years since. Alan, let's do this.

Three cherished friends invested financially in this project, and I pray their lives are enriched in every way in return. A special thank-you to Andrew Oates, Kurt O'Brien, and Todd Nichols.

This book has been field tested in two generations and two locations. To the original brain trust – my lifetime friends Brent Hardegree, Kevin Rhoads, and June Carter, as well as the people of Turning Point Community Church "back in the day," thank you for rolling with me on this. Then the coaching groups who tested these ideas in their own lives and work – Allison, Whitney, Brittany, Christina, Judson, Matt, Will, Chris, Kailee, Janice, Larry, Danielle, Marcy, Jim, Brenda, John, Susan M., Drew, Sara, James, Charity, Michael, C. J., Dale, Chelsea, Susan G., Steve, Janet, Mike and Amy – all of you provided real-time feedback and a rich level of engagement. You proved that LifeVesting works when you work it.

Foreword

I measure the value of a gift by the way it keeps on giving long after I've received it, and I measure the value of an investment by the return it generates for me over time.

Andy Wood has given both you and me a gift. *LifeVesting* is a resource you can use to create an investment: in yourself, the world around you, your future, and your eternity. The principles in this book are timeless and tested. I've seen them work again and again in my life and leadership, and they'll work for you as well.

Are you tired of limitations and failed expectations? *LifeVesting* points the way to a life of joyful abundance. I've been blessed enough to experience this abundance in my personal and professional life, and I believe in Andy's ability to help you get there too.

Do you have a burning desire to make a difference that lasts beyond your lifetime? You'll find a kindred spirit here. Andy's forty-plus years as an influencer can help you increase your impact and influence. He knows what he's talking about, and after you finish reading this book, so will you.

If you ever find yourself feeling bored or stagnant, you'll find in the pages of this book one growth idea after another. Read it a second time, and you'll find a whole new set of ideas lighting a fire in your imagination. That's the power of *LifeVesting*. Andy Wood is a soul on fire, and I hope you're ready to experience how he can ignite yours.

Are you stuck in habits, beliefs, or relationships that leave you yearning for freedom? You'll find here the tracks of a fellow struggler and hope for the breakthrough you're praying for. When I was a young man, I battled with depression and self-harm, never truly believing in myself. Just like Andy, I also found a way to let go of the prison that existed in my mind and in my life. His words will create a pathway for you to carve out that freedom we've both experienced.

Get ready to fan a flame burning inside you that not even death can extinguish. You've come to the right place for the inspiration, motivation, and drive to ignite the passion that's burning underneath the surface. Andy will help you tap into that energy to make your way down a new path that can help transform your life.

What you *won't* find here is a collection of platitudes from somebody who doesn't get it. Andy learned a long time ago that failure isn't fatal. And good choices today create multiplied benefits down the road. *LifeVesting* is a reminder that as long as you have life, you still have a choice. You still have an opportunity to grow into who you know you can be.

Picture this book as a "guide by your side"—coaching in print—exploring your dreams, relationships, and life challenges with you. Your investment is not in Andy's material but in using the principles here to cocreate the future and eternity you long for.

Andy has helped thousands find purpose, create value, and increase results. He has walked with people through seasons of unspeakable pain. He has helped others find freedom from brokenness and addiction. And he has shared insights that became turning points for untold lives. He's been a pastor, a teacher, a blogger, a leader, and an executive coach. What matters most to you, however, is that he's a friend. And what you'll find here is the sweet counsel and encouragement of someone who's *for* you and believes deeply *in* you.

I believe in you too.

Now it's your turn. Take the gift. Start making those investments. Your future abundance, impact, and freedom await.

—Kary Oberbrunner
CEO of Igniting Souls Publishing Agency
Wall Street Journal and *USA Today* best-selling author

And don't allow yourselves to be weary in planting good seeds, for the season of reaping the wonderful harvest you've planted is coming!
—Galatians 6:9, TPT

Introduction

Spent!

I don't know how else to describe it. I was spent.

Financially? Broke.

Emotionally? Discouraged.

Relationally? Lonely and isolated.

Physically? Constant exhaustion.

Can you relate?

What's crazy was that no one knew, because I had figured out how to fake it. Or superficially fix it. Oh . . . and I was making my living communicating truth to people about how they could live an "abundant" life. But I was like a penniless man offering investment advice. While the content may have been spot-on, I lacked the credibility and character to back it up.

I was a Christian pastor, living the life of a consumer. Despite what I knew in my head, the way I lived reflected the subtle belief that everything was up to me. Too proud to ask for help, too smart to admit how clueless I was, I built a life of running on fumes.

Spent.

And spent people can make galactically stupid choices.

Where was *my* abundant life Jesus said He came to give?

Where was the influence I had experienced in the past that now felt so fleeting?

What happened to the vibrant growth and transformation I had experienced earlier?

Why did I feel so bound up—a slave to past agreements and choices that held me captive, especially when I knew I was short of the freedom Christ had purchased for me?

Where was the heart that once pursued eternal values with passion?

Spent. It was all spent. I was like a kid who couldn't stand the rattling of change in his piggy bank without emptying it out. I settled for consuming chump change, when I knew—I *knew*—that God had more.

The Call That Changed It All

Along the way I went through an epic brokenness and restoration process. I experienced God's grace in amazing ways I never could have imagined. That's a story for another day. But I was alive again! Healing. Growing. Discovering new vistas of service and truth.

Yet some questions and frustrations remained. Why did everything still seem to take so long? Why did I feel as if I was still in catch-up mode? Why did God seem to be "doing things" for everybody else, but all my answers included the word *wait*? Why did my progress seem to feel like that old cliché of three steps forward and two steps back? Why did other people seem to be reaping their abundant harvest while I was still reaping the whirlwind?

Then one night the phone rang. My son, Joel, was working on an English essay during his freshman year in college.

"Dad," he said, "I'm thinking of an idea and I wanted you to help me."

His idea: take concepts of investing from the financial world and apply them to other areas of our lives.

"I'm calling it LifeVesting," he said.

"Sounds interesting," I said.

"I just need to know what other areas of life I should include," he went on.

We talked about several ways to approach his idea. Then we explored how to apply investment principles to these various life themes. This fascinated me because it combined two of my worlds. I'd worked in financial services for a brief period of my life, and, at that time, some facet of ministry for more than twenty-five years. We talked about risks and rewards, about seeking a return in various areas of our lives, and how *profit* isn't a dirty word. But mostly we talked about relationships—with God, others, and ourselves. Joel decided to focus on those three, calling them GodVesting, OtherVesting, and SelfVesting.

What started as my son's (very successful!) English paper became an ongoing dialogue between my son and me, and the Lord and me. Since then I've also had the opportunity to share these ideas with thousands of people around the world. People yearning to discover a life that gives more than it takes and energizes more than it exhausts. A life of freedom, joy, and abundance—not just in religious theory but in reality.

It's now my deep honor to share these ideas with you.

Who am I?

Just a guy who believes—with passion—that you can make choices today that will enrich your life tomorrow. But first you'll have to get your head out of that spending fog.

We live in a world of consumers—not only of goods and services in the economy but of lives as well. We consume our energy. We consume our friendships. We consume our health. We consume our religious practices. And we're told by the culture that consumption is somehow patriotic or virtuous. It's neither.

You only get one life, with all its promise and peril. Your life comes complete with a unique set of realities, rewards, and raw deals. Of opportunities and obstacles, friends and fiends. And did I mention choices? An endless array of choices. Some seem insignificant and mundane, others stressful and ominous. But every choice creates a set of consequences. You, my friend, will serve those consequences—or they will serve you.

LifeVesting is about taking charge of those choices. That starts with becoming intentional about what you want out of life. It's about shifting your focus from the immediate to infinity. Yet you don't have to sacrifice every bit of short-term happiness to make it happen.

LifeVesting is about your future and how to shape it.

LifeVesting is about your eternity and how to impact it.

LifeVesting is about your relationships and how to enrich them.

LifeVesting is about your dreams and how to experience them.

LifeVesting is about your legacy and how to leave one that lasts.

LifeVesting is about your influence and how to multiply it.

LifeVesting is about your freedom and how to walk in it.

LifeVesting is about a relationship with Jesus Christ and how to receive from Him as you advance His kingdom.

LifeVesting is about you and how you can live—really live—an abundant life.

Come with me on a journey—your journey—to a life rich in value, love, and immense joy.

How to Use this Book

Imagine you and I are sitting at a table, enjoying your favorite beverage, talking about life. Sometimes I'm doing the talking. But you'll have opportunities to write your story into the conversation as well. Don't waste those chances! Take time to add to this story; don't just (here's that word again) consume it.

Think of this book as a down payment. More value is coming. The book functions as an idea generator. *Your* idea generator. What you read and how you apply it becomes an investment in *your* life and legacy. Goose-steppers, groupies, and clones need not apply.

This book is the beginning of the dialogue of ideas, not the final word on anything. If you merely read it and move on to the next book, you will have missed the point. That would be like reading a book about Disney World but never actually going to the Magic Kingdom.

Think of the chapters that follow as a field guide. Each contains five sections and two ways to navigate through it. You may prefer to take the chapter as a whole or engage each section at a time as a daily study. Throughout the chapters you will discover general principles, biblical truths, and lots of stories. This book contains truth that can change your life and destiny—but only if you do something with it.

If you're an average reader, each section is a quick read. But each chapter challenges you to go deeper than that, to use your Bible and your brain as well. There are plenty of scripture references. Take the time to actually look them up. You will doubtless see insights I didn't, and you'll profit immensely from the discipline of doing that.

If you were starting or expanding a business, you might need some financial help to make it happen. That help is called "seed money." LifeVestors need seed sources too, but our seeds are *ideas*. So following each section, I've tossed a few seeds your way and given you some space to . . . well, invest. To think, to pray, to journal, to dream. So slow down. Reflect. Plant those seeds in your heart.

I've had a few "adventures of a lifetime." I hope you have too. But I'm at a point in my life where I'm ready for my lifetime to *be* the adventure. Not just for my consumption but for a generation to come. And for the honor of the One who calls us to the greatest adventure of all—cheating the grave and living forever.

I want to be a LifeVestor.

Let's do it together.

Andy Wood
Millry, Alabama

CHAPTER 1

When Your Life Becomes an Investment

Kimmerer, Wyoming. Let me introduce you to Jim, co-owner and operator of the Golden Rule dry goods store. He was hardly the first businessman to ever try to operate by the Golden Rule, but he was one of the few to put the words on his door. And the fact that Jim and his wife lived across the street from their store made it even more vital to practice what he preached.

One night Jim and his wife were awakened by a loud banging at their door. A Chinese man who spoke no English, gesturing wildly, beckoned Jim to open his store.

What would you do? Point to a clock and ask the man to come back when the big hand got there, and the little hand got there? Close the door and go back to bed? Call the police?

Jim put himself in the place of his manic visitor and chose a different path. He changed to his day clothes, lit a lamp, and crossed the dark street. Once inside his shop, Jim marveled as the stranger went from shelf to shelf, looking for a specific item. Finally the Chinese man found a white nightgown hanging from the ceiling and bought it.

Applying the Golden Rule again, Jim offered to wrap the purchase. His guest refused but did insist that the store owner follow him around the corner to his own laundry shop.

Golden Rule time again. Jim followed his new friend and entered the laundry shop, where a man sat in the back, writhing in pain. He was dying, and soon. Together Jim and the Chinese host dressed the ailing man in the white garment. Then Mr. Golden Rule finally returned home, wondering why a man would want to wear a female nightgown.

The next day Jim learned the old man had died in the night. He later discovered why his late-night customer was so insistent. According to Chinese tradition, dressing in white was necessary to enter the presence of ancestors upon passing. He later remarked of the experience, "I learned how much people want to be treated just as people. I, in turn, had the chance to do a service."

What Jim called Golden Rule service, I refer to as LifeVesting. This devoted Christian man demonstrated how choices we make today can add great value to others now, and to our own lives in the future. This story, like many others, reflects a timeless set of principles and an economy designed by no less than God Himself. In this chapter we'll explore some of those foundational principles.

The Simplest Budget in the World

For eighteen years I lived in Lubbock, Texas, home of Texas Tech, tumbleweeds, and flat tires. No kidding. In Lubbock when the wind starts blowing, tires start blowing too. Apparently the wind exposes nails and screws on the road, and the results are predictable.

Whenever one of our cars got that sinking feeling, there was no question what to do. We called Flores Tire. Let me tell you why.

When babies are born, God gives them a voice and lungs to sound the alarm when they have a need. The only word they know is "Whaaaaa," but it works pretty well.

When babies go to college, only the vocabulary changes.

"Dad," Carrie said on the phone one day in a whimpering voice, "I have a flaaaaatt!"

(Sigh.) "Where are you?"

"I'm at Spanky's near the Tech campus." Translation: on the other side of town.

"Okay. I'll be there as quick as I can."

I wove through the grid and traffic light maze and found my daughter in the restaurant parking lot. She had that look. If you've ever been the parent of a teenager, I need not say more, but for the rest of you, it was the I'm-sorry-I-know-this-is-a-lot-of-trouble look.

The biggest trouble was trying to figure out where they hid the jack.

I sat in the passenger's seat of Carrie's little red car, searching the owner's manual and muttering to myself. When I looked up, there he was. I don't remember his name—let's call him Anthony. He was driving an oversized pickup with an air compressor and a bunch of tools on the back.

"Would you like me to change that for you?" he asked.

Imagine me smiling. A lot.

"Sure," I said.

Anthony didn't just offload the flat and replace it with that tire wannabe lodged in the trunk. He found out what was wrong with it (a nail) and fixed it. All onsite. I never knew such a business existed. All the while, I was pumping him with questions. No, he was not the owner. Yes, they could go anywhere in town. Yes, they're available 24/7.

Finally, the ultimate question: "How much do I owe you?"

"Nothing," he said. "Next time you need us, give us a call. And recommend us to your friends."

With that, he handed me a few business cards. And I handed him a promise: "I sure will!"

I took one of those cards and as I left went even further out of my way. I wanted to meet the owner of Flores Tire. I wanted to find the man who would empower an employee to solve people's problems on his dime. I wanted to tell him I'd be back, that I'd be calling again.

And call I have. Every single time I've had a need. With five cars and a lot of home construction in the area, believe me, we've had a lot of need.

The guys at Flores Tire personify success in any dimension. They're *LifeVestors*. Why? *They do more than they have to, more often than they want to, for less money than they deserve.* But they do it with a greater view in mind. They believe the little extras today can create large dividends tomorrow. As you will see, that's a principle seen throughout the Bible.

One act of kindness in a restaurant parking lot more than paid for itself many times over. It wasn't the size of the sacrifice—Anthony's kindness took about thirty minutes, and I saved $22.50. It was the fact that he was willing to go the second mile to meet someone's needs *today*, and gladly settle for getting the reward *tomorrow*. That's what LifeVestors do. They create opportunities, and those opportunities create the potential for amazing benefits down the road.

Anthony and the company owner also understood something about the use of time and money. In the final analysis, there are four things on which you can spend any of your resources. Four and only four. No matter how many financial categories you track, just four. No matter how many ways you spend your time, it still comes down to four things:

Yesterday. Today. Tomorrow. Eternity.

That's it. Take any expenditure of time or money, energy or esteem, love or language. You'll find it falls into one of those four categories. Anything else is just details.

Yesterday spending refers to those obligations you made in the past that you're still paying for. Yesterday's purchases. Yesterday's promises. Yesterday's pain. These are your debts, and I don't mean money only.

Today spending refers to those desires and needs you encounter daily. Gas and groceries. Gifts and games with your kids. Utilities and underwear.

Tomorrow spending? Those are the resources you save and invest to serve your needs later in the future. Initiative and investing. Retirement and redirection, such as downsizing. Replacement purchases such as washing machines or furniture.

Eternity spending has to do with what you give. Your church and charitable giving. Your service and your smile. Your faith, hope, and love.

Would it surprise you to know that most of our lives are aimed at yesterday and today? In fact, the success of the American economy depends on keeping money in circulation. That means getting you to spend money you don't have on things you don't need. Am I the only one who gets nervous about that? Or that the average total household debt in the US is more than twice our median disposable annual income? The same is true for relationships. We've come to recognize people as consumables—worth keeping while they're useful, then we toss them and move on.

LifeVesting is about re-aiming your life toward your future and your eternity. Not just in your finances but in every area of your life. It's about establishing a treasure, both in heaven (see Matthew 6:19) and in your earthly tomorrows.

The Bible and life are filled with examples of LifeVestors. That superwoman mentioned in Proverbs 31? A LifeVestor. She thinks ahead and manages her money and time so that she laughs at the future (see Proverbs 31:25).

King David was a LifeVestor too (see 1 Chronicles 29). He invested enormous sums of money for the construction of a temple that wouldn't even bear his name.

But the ultimate LifeVestor is the Lord Jesus himself. He lived it. Taught it. And made it possible for us to be LifeVestors too.

Becoming a LifeVestor involves three things: (1) Take an honest look at how you spend your resources. (2) Find out where your "treasure" is today (that may surprise you), and where you want it to be. (3) Realign your life to pursue your treasure. That means saying no to some of the whims and desires of today so you can choose to invest in the future and the hope God has said was His intention for all of us (see Jeremiah 29:11).

"As long as it is day, we must do the works of him who sent me," Jesus said. "Night is coming, when no one can work" (John 9:4, NIV). LifeVestors recognize the principle that you don't have forever to work. But you *will* have forever (and probably a long time on the planet) to live with the results of what you did or didn't do.

Decide to be a LifeVestor. Do more than you have to. Do it more often than you want to. For a season you may receive less reward than you deserve. But if you do it with a larger view in mind, down the road it will be more than worth it.

And if you're ever in Lubbock, Texas, riding on your rims, call Flores Tire on Clovis Highway. They're worth it too.

SEED MONEY

1. What dreams, projects, relationships, or needs do you have that require you to do "more than you have to, more often than you want to, for less reward than you deserve"? How do you feel about it? Discouraged? Hopeful?

2. Draw a pie chart that shows how you proportion the different areas of your life among the four "budget items"—yesterday, today, tomorrow, and eternity. Unsure? Start by looking at how you spend your money. Then how you spend your time.

3. Read 1 Chronicles 29:1–20. What insights do you see here about how LifeVestors think and act?

4. What one change could you make in your life today that would move you closer to the vision you described in question 1?

Not Everyone Is a LifeVestor

That must have been some party. It's amazing the bash somebody can throw when the only invited guest is his own soul. No evidence here of wine, women, or keeping the neighbors up. Just a self-congratulating dance in the head of somebody who's been very successful . . . and assumes it'll always be that way. Here's the story:

> Then he said, "Beware! Guard against every kind of greed. Life is not measured by how much you own."
> Then he told them a story: "A rich man had a fertile farm that produced fine crops. He said to himself, 'What should I do? I don't have

room for all my crops.' Then he said, 'I know! I'll tear down my barns and build bigger ones. Then I'll have room enough to store all my wheat and other goods. And I'll sit back and say to myself, "My friend, you have enough stored away for years to come. Now take it easy! Eat, drink, and be merry!"'

"But God said to him, 'You fool! You will die this very night. Then who will get everything you worked for?'

"Yes, a person is a fool to store up earthly wealth but not have a rich relationship with God."

Luke 12:15–21, NLT

Here was a man who assumed there would always be a tomorrow. His treasure was completely wrapped up in himself and what he could hoard. And he gambled and lost when God came collecting.

It's one thing to prepare for the future. It's another to presume you'll have time or to ignore the eternal consequences of your choices. When the world's keeping score, none of us are guaranteed that "success" implies wisdom. Today's hero can become tomorrow's has-been.

One way to understand LifeVesting is to define it in terms of what it *isn't*. LifeVestors have counterfeits and alter egos, and rich or not by the world's standards, a fool is a fool. Just as there are only four things you can spend your resources on, there are four foolish ways to throw your life away.

CONSUMERS

Consumers focus almost exclusively on *today*. Users and takers, they spend their money, time, and relationships on immediate wants and needs. Consumers focus mainly on themselves. They don't always intend to be selfish, but they're guided by "What's in it for me?" They come to church for what they can get out of it. They spend their resources in ways that, when spent, are gone forever.

For consumers no other moment exists but now. Tomorrow will take care of itself. Somehow. Magically. Like Scarlett O'Hara, they'll worry about the details and tough choices tomorrow. Like the rich fool, they're sure the sun'll come up tomorrow, as it did today.

Everybody has immediate needs, but consumers build their lives around theirs. They can't seem to define or even consider the long-term consequences of their decisions. So they spend away their time, money, relationships, and energy—faster than it comes in. When they run out of their own resources, they don't stop there. They use up somebody else's resources.

At best, consumers are always running on empty themselves. They're frustrated when they can't have what they want, when they want it. At their worst, they become users and leeches. They drain the resources and energy of those around them. They aren't bad people; they've just learned to define their self-worth by their ability to get what they want right now.

HOARDERS

It's one thing to save for the future or conserve energy or money. Hoarders, on the other hand, avoid risk at all cost and avoid sharing any more than necessary. They have no time, no money, no love to give. Many hoarders inherited a spirit of poverty through a profoundly stressful experience. Have you ever listened to someone who lived through the Great Depression or grew up "dirt poor"? Often their circumstances have changed a lot, but their *perceptions* haven't. By fearing another season of loss, they live in poverty of soul. Others become relationship hoarders because someone they trusted betrayed them in the past. They've decided that love, friendship, and trust are too risky.

Jesus gave a great example of a hoarding mentality in His story of the talents (see Matthew 25:14–30). A wealthy man entrusts varying amounts of money to three servants to manage. These "talents" were worth about $250,000–$500,000 apiece in today's currency. Two servants did well, doubling their master's money. The other was a hoarder. Check out his reasoning: "I knew you were a hard man, and I was afraid you would rob me of what I earned, so I hid your money in the earth and here it is!" (v. 24, TLB). Now that's something every boss wants to hear!

Hoarders aren't thieves or consumers. They're counterfeit investors. Like Life-Vestors, hoarders have an eye on the future. But like that reluctant servant, they base their decisions on fear of the future and a false view of God. It's not that they do bad things—they don't do anything at all. *To avoid risk, they avoid everything.* Jesus described them tersely: "wicked and lazy." Ouch!

GAMBLERS

Gamblers look for a quick fix. They shoot from the hip and want results in a hurry. They're as addicted to the chase as to the actual prize itself. That's why when they win, they often gamble it all away again.

Like hoarders, gamblers can look like LifeVestors. That's because they're willing to take action despite the often-heavy risks involved. But there is a difference. LifeVestors take action based on a reasonable expectation of results. *And they're willing to stick with a good decision until they reap the benefits.*

Are there risks? Sure. Sometimes unforeseen circumstances occur. Sometimes the environment or the weather or people change. Sometimes even the Lord withholds results as a form of testing.

Gamblers are different. They act with no predictable idea whatsoever of the possible results. They define "the future" by hours, not months or years. Their expectations of gain are not based on wisdom or sound experience but on feelings or whims.

In short, gamblers are adrenaline junkies. They're often restless and rootless in their relationships. Their biggest enemy—boredom. Their biggest fear—the lack of change.

Are you a life gambler or a LifeVestor? Here's a quick way to tell: *are you willing to wait for the results you want when you're confident you've made the right decisions?* That's too dull for most speculators. They need action—even if means hurting a lot of people.

PLEASERS

Pleasers use their resources to buy love or approval. They look responsible and generous. But pleasers give out of an unhealthy desire to "fix" someone they love or rescue them from a crisis. Pleasers get a lot of satisfaction from their ability to give freely. They give time, money, forgiveness, and complete devotion. They need to be needed, and when the need appears, they give and love and serve with total abandon.

But wait. Aren't we supposed to love unconditionally? Yes. But not at the expense of serving the greater needs of those we love. Sometimes the worst thing you can do is rescue someone from a bad choice.

Aren't we supposed to give generously? Sure. But not at the expense of having something left to offer the Lord and the world later. If you keep giving with reckless abandon, the day will come when you have nothing left to offer. And God help the giver who has nothing left to give!

Aren't we supposed to love deeply? Yes. But not at the expense of seeking first the kingdom of God (see Matthew 6:33). You can't love your neighbor or yourself if you're not offering Jesus your first love. And *sooner or later, first love to Jesus will lead you to say no to somebody you desperately want to please.*

At any given time, you can choose to be a consumer, hoarder, gambler, or pleaser. No one is immune. Most likely when you do, you'll be unaware of it. It takes courage and humility to take a hard look at your life-wasting patterns. But until you do, you risk living the life of a fool.

SEED MONEY

1. What's the difference between the way the world "keeps score" (money, power, pleasure, etc.) and the way God does? In which areas of your life God would tell you "Well done"? What areas do you need to work on?

2. When you're not in "LifeVesting" mode, which of the four "alter-egos" do you tend to drift into? How do you see each of these patterns in the various areas of your life?

3. Take another look at Luke 12:16–21. Jesus said that "life is not measured by how much you own." Then how is your life measured, according to these verses?

4. Name one action (keep it simple) you can take in the next twenty-four hours to move out of your preferred "alter-ego" mode.

The LifeVesting Cycle

We experience life in a variety of cycles. Weather patterns, economic cycles, and that calendar on your wall come to mind. LifeVesting is no different. When you give yourself to a compelling future, you pass through different seasons. Each season calls for different choices and actions. Those choices and actions take you from where you are to where you want to go.

Getting to your desired destination requires a good GPS. Here that stands for Goal Positioning System. Or maybe God Pursuing System. In this section we'll explore a framework that lets you know you're moving forward and what happens next.

Don't think of these as a locked-in sequence of steps. Instead, think of the LifeVesting cycle as a *flow* of activity, moving from one stage to another. The Bible uses different metaphors to show this, but in this case, I'll stick with farming. When you decide to experience a "harvest" of your "investment," how does that flow from one stage to the next?

STAGE 1: EXPLORE THE POSSIBILITIES

> *He who goes to and fro weeping, carrying his bag of seed,*
> *Shall indeed come again with a shout of joy, bringing his sheaves*
> *with him.*
>
> Psalm 126:6

First-century farmers planted in a way we would consider backward. In those days the farmer would cast his seed first, then plow it in and cultivate the ground. Not very efficient by today's standards, but the spiritual image is compelling. Once the farmer had a vision of what he wanted to harvest, he prepared to cast the seed. He didn't take soil samples or analyze the land to death. He walked back and forth, looking for opportunities to cast.

In this stage of LifeVesting, you consider the kind of results you want to have by doing what our farmer did here. Walk around. Think. Pray. Dream. Imagine. Discover. Ask, "What if . . . ?" Then ask it again. Nearly everything of value that has ever been created started with this step. Someone dared to explore the possibilities.

STAGE 2: FOLLOW YOUR PASSION

> *Those who go out weeping,*
> *carrying seed to sow,*
> *will return with songs of joy,*
> *carrying sheaves with them.*
>
> Psalm 126:5, NIV

What *moves* you? *Burdens* you? *Breaks your heart*? Until you answer the passion question, you've yet to find what it takes to truly invest your life in a desired result. Your "harvest" should matter enough that you would weep over it, work for it, or sing in celebration when you reach it. Don't assume you can calculate a formula, start the machine, then sit and watch the returns roll in. This is your *life* we're talking about!

If you've yet to get the memo, read it here: *you're going to be tested*. Can you still act decisively when you're exhausted to tears? Will you keep doing the next right thing, even when it looks impossible? Will you refuse to take no for an answer? In God's kingdom, if you can "take it or leave it," God will leave it every time.

STAGE 3: ALLOCATE YOUR RESOURCES

You can't plant if you don't have any seeds. You can't invest if you've squandered all your resources. George Clason's classic book *The Richest Man in Babylon* revolves around a simple discipline: "A portion of all I earn is mine to keep." I would change that to say, a part of all you receive is yours to multiply. But you must choose to do it. So save some money, carve out some time, spare some energy for the next life investment. If you spend all your resources on yesterday and today, you are sabotaging your future.

LifeVestors first decide what results they want. Then they begin gathering and channeling their resources toward making it happen. The great news is that you don't have to start with an abundance—just a little, with time, consistency, and action. The even better news—you don't have to do this alone. You live in a world of abundant resources and people willing to help you.

STAGE 4: EXECUTE YOUR PLAN

It's not enough to create the idea, carry the burden, or carve out the resources. Sooner or later you have to *decide*, to *dare*, to *do*. Planning is important, but only if you execute the plan. Dreaming is powerful, but only if you take the first step toward turning it into reality. Make the call, write the letter, go to lunch with whomever.

It's in the execution that most of us figure out we're dealing with more than one aspect of our lives. The most authentic life investments involve more than just throwing money at something. They also call for your time, relationships, and abilities.

Over time, wise LifeVestors learn that some plans are better than others. Some may be worthy of a nod, while others are that "pearl of great value" (see Matthew 13:45–46). Sometimes we even learn to ask, "Where'd *that* crazy idea come from?" But there's no substitute for bold action. Even when that action risks failure, rejection, or disappointment.

STAGE 5: PROTECT YOUR INVESTMENT

Want to see a farmer laugh? Tell him you're going to plant corn or tomatoes, take a three-month vacation, and come back to pick your harvest. It doesn't work that way. Investments of any type call for care and cultivation. Jesus' story of the sower (see Matthew 13:3–9, 18–23) shows how rare a harvest can be. The seed that fell on the hard path became birdseed. The seed that fell on stony ground or among the thorns grew up rootless and choked, respectively.

Investments—seeds of all types and the environment they're planted in—need nourishing. In farm-speak that means three things. You break up the hard, resistant places. You deepen the shallow places. You pull the weeds. In practical terms that means identifying the things in your environment that hinder your success and overcoming them. Did I mention this is work? Where every day hurls new surprises and challenges? But if the harvest is worth it, then the cultivating is worthwhile.

STAGE 6: ENLARGE YOUR CAPACITY

What do you suppose God wants to do with that believer who sees some measure of success? Here's one answer:

> *"He lops off every branch that doesn't produce. And he prunes those branches that bear fruit for even larger crops."*
>
> John 15:2, TLB

Think about this. God wants to enlarge successful LifeVestors to become even more successful! And in case you're wondering what Jesus means by "prunes," the writer of Hebrews refers to this as *discipline*. And discipline is hard—even sorrowful (see Hebrews 12:11). But it's worth it in the end.

Pruning looks painful to the tree or vine. At first it appears to reverse the plant's growth. But the long-term result is graceful, powerful, beautiful. It works for LifeVestors too. God is still writing your life story. And as He does, He deepens your capacity to love, lengthens your capacity to endure, and enlarges your capacity to receive. Painful? Yes. But purposeful. And worth it.

STAGE 7: GIVE IT TIME

There is no substitute for time. And the larger the investment, the longer the wait. It takes forty days to make a squash, forty years to make an oak tree. How long do you suppose it takes to fulfill *your* potential?

I don't wait well. I like to see visible results, and soon! I have to remember that like the oak tree the most important growth goes undetected for a long time.

I also have a bias for action, and that's good news. As we'll explore later, waiting doesn't mean sitting around doing nothing.

Care to guess the most significant thing you can do while you're waiting for results? You cycle back around and start exploring the possibilities again. Where do you go from here, once you achieve the goal or realize the vision?

What I have described here isn't limited to one LifeVesting "element." You may move through several of these cycles in different areas of your life simultaneously. And each cycle is at a different stage. The key to moving forward is awareness. You have to know where you are and how the Lord is moving in the process. It's also important to align yourself with principles that make or break your results. That's the topic of our next section.

SEED MONEY

1. Imagine a "blue sky world," where you're experiencing one dream come true after another. How could your life be different a year from now? Five or ten years from now?

2. Read Matthew 13:3–9, 18–23. Each type of ground describes a type of heart that God's truth can land upon. What kind of "ground" best describes your heart? What do you think God is doing to make your life more fruitful?

3. Pick a significant goal, dream, or relationship in your life. Where do you think you are in the LifeVesting cycle, related to that? What does that suggest to you about your next course of action?

4. Now pick one action step that would move you from where you are now toward the next stage in the LifeVesting cycle.

The Five Laws of LifeVesting

Ever get the feeling that you're pushing a giant boulder up a long hill? Every step gets harder, more dangerous. At other times do you feel as though you're riding a huge wave of momentum, where every step forward feels easy?

What's the difference? Alignment. God has established an ordered world based on eternal principles or laws found in His Word. The more you align your life with those principles, the more you experience the fullness of God's purpose. You move through growth stages faster. Relationships form at deeper levels. Your influence grows. And you experience more personal freedom.

In this ordered world, *everything begins with and culminates in the glory of God.* You and I were created to express His image, extend His life, and execute His will. And to fulfill that purpose, we were given the awesome gift of one lifetime.

That's it. No plan B. No second chances as a toad or platypus. You get one shot, with no guarantees of how long that will be. But with that one lifetime, you get to make something happen. You can produce consequences affecting your future, in both time and eternity. You can also create a lasting impact on other lives, including generations yet to be born.

LifeVesting is about understanding those possibilities and moving toward your compelling future. It all revolves around five biblical principles. You find them expressed in a variety of images—agriculture, business, family relationships, even fishing. But the principles are consistent, regardless of the metaphor. This is an invitation to get A LIFE!

A—THE PRINCIPLE OF ABUNDANCE

> *I live in an abundant universe, created by an abundant God,*
> *who wants me to have an abundant life.*

Throughout scripture God reveals himself as a God of abundance. Whatever He does, He does abundantly. He gives abundantly. He loves abundantly. He heals abundantly. He saves abundantly. What He offers us is more than enough, far beyond anything we could ever ask or imagine. We're limited only by our capacity to receive.

Why, then, don't we receive abundantly from the Lord? Because we close ourselves off from Him. Or we're limited in our faith or focus. This leads to *scarcity thinking*—the belief that there is only so much blessing to go around.

When we're unwilling to wait or endure, that also hurts our capacity to receive. Settling too quickly for the cheap and easy superficial leads to a limited, superficial life.

Also, some blessings only come as the result of fighting for them. It can be frightening to risk rejection by pushing back against the culture or doing something unpopular but necessary. But when you give in to the fear, by default you give up on abundance.

One more thing. If you try to combine God's abundance with your glory, you'll run into a brick wall. God doesn't share His glory with anyone.

L—THE PRINCIPLE OF LEADERSHIP

I have the potential to influence others both in this life
and long after my life on earth is over.

Even if you don't think of yourself as a leader, you are. Everybody influences somebody. Someone looks to you as the person to obey, example to follow, partner to collaborate with, or sense-maker in times of uncertainty or confusion.

Sometimes people imitate you. Or they reflect on something you said. Sometimes they follow you and your life choices. Sometimes they buy, try, or avoid things because of your suggestions or mistakes.

Leadership may take a lot of work. At other times you can influence others with little to no effort. Sometimes you influence people and know it. Often you remain oblivious to it. Sometimes you're on a public stage. But you can also shake the earth with potential, even when you're not in front of a crowd.

Your choices, words, attitudes, and direction sway others one way or another. And this isn't limited to your earthly lifetime. Here's a fascinating description of the life of Abel: "By faith Abel still speaks, even though he is dead" (Hebrews 11:4, NIV). Abel's life and faith, even though he never uttered a word that was quoted in scripture, lives to this day. Yours can live on as well.

I—THE PRINCIPLE OF INCREASE

I was created to be fruitful and multiply in every dimension of life.

The purpose of investing is to increase the value of the original investment. That's true in the financial realm and in LifeVesting. As I invest my time, love, respect, or resources, I receive a multiplied increase. The parable of the sower (see Mark 4:1–8) speaks of various levels of profit. So does the parable of the talents. The parable of the vine (see John 15:1–8) says that God will prune my life to make it more fruitful. These all reflect the law of the harvest—I reap *what* I sow, *later* than I sow, *more* than I sow.

This makes some Christians nervous. We're supposed to do what we do for the privilege of humble service and nothing more. Aren't we?

Not so fast. Jesus often spoke about rewards, both in this life and in the age to come. Nearly every New Testament writer did the same. They challenged believers to make choices today that would reward them in the future.

Growth—increase—is a sign of life and health. You often experience that in measurable terms, like money, time, or the size of an organization. Sometimes, though, you experience increase in less tangible ways, such as relationships. When you invest in a quality relationship, that friendship or partnership can greatly increase the quality of your entire life.

F—THE PRINCIPLE OF FREEDOM

*Wise choices today will provide the freedom to have
more choices available in the future.*

God gives us money as a tangible way to practice stewardship in all the areas of economy (see Luke 16:11). Because it's so measurable, it's easy to see the idea of financial freedom. Here's how it works. I put part of my income to work for a season while I am still able to work to earn it. If I continue to do that, then the day will come when instead of working for my money, my money is working for me.

But the principle of freedom doesn't stop there. It applies to relationships, both personal and business. It applies to wisdom and worship, work and warfare. We give today in order to receive when we have little else to give. We serve today so when we need it most, others will gladly serve our needs. In the natural that means retirement or redirection. In the spiritual it refers to eternal life.

This is illustrated in the story of the unrighteous steward (see Luke 16:1–9). Though he was unrighteous, the steward was shrewd. When faced with having to give an account for his poor performance, he wised up. He prepared for "life on the other side" by being kind and generous to his master's debtors.

E—THE PRINCIPLE OF ETERNITY

The quality of my eternity depends on the choices I make in this life.

You and I have an eternal destiny, shaped by our choices. "How does a man benefit," Jesus asked, "if he gains the whole world and loses his soul in the process?" (Mark 8:36, TLB). *Nothing else in this book has any relevance to you if you do not have a personal relationship with Jesus Christ.* LifeVesting is not about performing or planning your way into heaven. You can't plan or invest away your sin problem. Only by faith in Jesus Christ can you experience the hope that comes through a relationship with God.

Jesus has already made the most significant eternal investment. He invested His death and resurrection in you. Your response is to acknowledge your need for Him, turn away from your sin, and receive Him as your Lord and Savior. From that moment you begin a forever relationship with God! Jesus put it this way. "Whoever hears my word and believes him who sent me has eternal life and will not be judged but has crossed over from death to life" (John 5:24, NIV).

Will LifeVesting principles work without a relationship with Jesus? Only in a temporary shadow form. They may help you gain the world. But in the face of eternity, that's chump change. Everything changes when you invest your life on the foundation of faith in Jesus. Then the choices you make can produce gains that will benefit you for all eternity.

Abundance. Leadership. Increase. Freedom. Eternity. These five laws are in operation whether you align with them or not. They reflect God's economy, where He wants you to be wealthy! You'll see the key to that in the next section.

SEED MONEY

1. Take another look at the parable of the talents in Matthew 25:14–30. Jesus said the landowner held His servants accountable for how abundantly they lived. What does that suggest to you about God's expectations for you and me? Based on this passage, what's the difference between abundance thinking and scarcity thinking?

2. Where do you see specific examples of abundance thinking in your own life? Where do you see scarcity thinking?

3. Make a list of at least seven people who are in your "influence zone." What are some specific ways you can "let your light shine" as an example to them?

4. Choose three areas of your life where you would like to experience multiplied growth. What specific changes would you like to see, by when?

God's Economy and Your Life Currency

It was the Beverly Hills of ancient Asia. A medical haven and center of wealth and high-end commerce. If you told your mama you got a job there, she'd be bragging about it the next day. This was some place. And there was a church in town.

One day Jesus sent a letter to the First Church of Coolville, alias Laodicea. Let's peek at their mail:

> *"I know your deeds, that you are neither cold nor hot. I wish you were either one or the other! So, because you are lukewarm—neither hot nor cold—I am about to spit you out of my mouth. You say, 'I am rich; I have acquired wealth and do not need a thing.' But you do not realize that you are wretched, pitiful, poor, blind and naked. I counsel you to buy from me gold refined in the fire, so you can become rich; and white clothes to wear, so you can cover your shameful nakedness; and salve to put on your eyes, so you can see."*

> Revelation 3:15–18

Looks like the guys and dolls in Lala Land had a few things to learn about wealth. So do we. They thought they were loaded; Jesus said otherwise. Yet in His love Jesus gave them, and LifeVestors everywhere, a few pointers on His economy.

We limit ourselves when we assume that God is only interested in "religious" things. We set ourselves up for disaster when we allow the world to define value or wealth.

If we can learn to operate our lives by His economy, we can experience extraordinary results. Here are ten key principles that govern God's system of wealth exchange.

Principle #1:
The root nature of sin is a declaration of independence from God.

That's been true since the days of Eden, even among believers. The Laodiceans were so blessed, they assumed they needed nothing. Not even God? Apparently not. Somewhere, somehow, their gratitude had turned to smugness. And Jesus was on the outside, knocking on the door of His own church (see Revelation 3:20).

Principle #2:
God has a system of economy unlike the world's system.

"You say you're rich," He said. "I say you're broke." And when God says you're busted, guess what? You're busted! It doesn't matter how the world keeps score. God has a different way to measure wealth and poverty, and it's more anchored to the truth, His truth.

Principle #3:
"Economy" is the exchange of all the commodities of life.

What do you think of when you hear the word *economy*? If you're like most people, you usually assume someone is talking about cash and coins. But the idea of economy is much larger than that. It has to do with how *everything*—tangible and intangible—is given and received, bought and sold. With that in mind, here are eight types of LifeVesting currency:

Leadership. This includes both authority and influence.

Money. You can be a LifeVestor with little money, but you can't be a LifeVestor with bad money management.

Insight. God intended wisdom to remain in circulation. That's why they call it "the wisdom of the ages."

Ability. No one can do everything, but everybody can do something. When you use your abilities to make a difference in someone else's life, you're using the currency of a LifeVestor.

Esteem. Another word for honor or respect. When you give away esteem, you invest in your own future as well as the future of those who desperately need it.

Love. Love gives. It takes deliberate action to seek another's well-being, regardless of the cost.

Words. LifeVestors use the power of words to awaken, heal, and encourage others.

Time. Your time is your life on a calculator. What you do with it reflects who or what you think is important and determines your destiny.

These eight currencies have a lasting and eternal quality about them. They span the realms of heaven and earth. Readily seen and used here on earth, they also are wonderfully used in worship there in heaven:

> *Saying with a loud voice,*
> *"Worthy is the Lamb that was slain to receive power [leadership]*
> *and riches and wisdom [insight] and might [ability] and honor [esteem]*
> *and glory [love] and blessing [words] . . . forever and ever [time]."*
>
> Revelation 5:11–13

Principle #4:
Money has a unique place in the commodities of life.

Jesus said that money was at the bottom of the ladder, inferior to every other resource (see Luke 16:10–11). It's also a false god; Jesus said categorically that you cannot serve God and money (see Luke 16:13). Your use of money also reveals what you truly value. "Where your treasure is," Jesus said, "there your heart will be also" (Matthew 6:21, NIV).

Principle #5:
It is possible to be rich in the world's economy and bankrupt in God's.

I don't want to beat this to death, but it's staggering how blinding this can be. This church in Laodicea didn't have a care in the world, and their wealth was the reason why. They had wallowed out a comfort zone that enabled them to continue "doing church." All the while they were exposed in the spiritual realm as "wretched, pitiful, poor, blind and naked." Their wealth itself was not the problem; it was their attitude toward it. Their complacency had marginalized their need for God.

Principle #6:
God wants us to be wealthy, according to His system of economy.

Lest you think that God is a cosmic killjoy, take another look at His heart toward these people. "I counsel you to buy from me gold refined in the fire, *so you can become rich*" (Revelation 3:18, NIV). If economy is the exchange of all the commodities of life, then maybe God wants us to experience it all! Not just toys and trinkets. Not just invisible spiritual wealth. All of it.

Principle #7:
We can only be wealthy in God's eyes when God is the source of our wealth.

The focus of the Laodiceans was on themselves. After a cold wake-up call, Jesus responds, "Let *Me* be your source." God is echoing the sentiment of Solomon. "The blessing of the LORD makes rich, and he adds no sorrow with it" (Proverbs 10:22, ESV). It's more important that you're blessed than that you're financially prosperous. The Lord is not as concerned with how much money you have as He is how much of *you* that money has.

Principle #8:
God uses needs to teach us to trust in Him.

He has promised to meet all your needs, according to His riches in glory in Christ (see Philippians 4:19). Your need is evidence of God's available provision. Yes, it requires you to let go of your pride and self-sufficiency. But in return you receive the gracious provision of the source of all wealth.

Principle #9:
The way to receive God's provision is to buy from God.

"I counsel you," Jesus says, "to buy from Me." Does that not strike you as odd? How do people who are penniless buy anything from God? Let me illustrate. Suppose I want a gallon of milk. I go to the grocery store, grab the goods, and start to leave. But before I can get out the door, I have to trade what I *have* (money) for what I *want* (milk). So what did these people have?

Their nothingness. And that's all God wanted. He wanted them to exchange their nothingness for His provision, at their point of need. Declare your need, in faith, with an open hand, and all the resources of heaven are brought to your situation.

Principle #10:
The practical way to buy from God is to give at your point of need.

Receiving in God's economy is the result of giving (see Luke 6:38). If you need money, give money. If you need love or friendship, give love or friendship. If you need more energy, you'll get more by exercising (giving) than by sleeping it off.

Try it. As you think through your goals and desired future, examine them in light of God's system of economy. How can you "buy from God" by giving at your point of need? How can you turn to Him as your source of wealth? How can you trust His heart to provide an abundant life as you learn to trust Him completely?

SEED MONEY

1. Give an example of how you could use each type of "currency" to invest in the future or eternity. Be as specific as possible.

2. "God wants us to be wealthy, according to His system of economy." Dig deeper into this principle. What would God want you to experience as blessing that you haven't fully realized yet? Think about measurable things as well as spiritual or immeasurable things.

3. Read Luke 6:27–38. According to these verses, what actions can you take that will change your destiny or someone else's?

4. Pick one of those actions you listed above. How and when can you act on that in the next week?

FINAL THOUGHT

Back to Jim, Mr. Golden Rule. You never know when you may have the opportunity to do a service. But you'll only have such rich opportunities when you extend kindness and care beyond the limits of your convenience and comfort zones.

What if something like that happened today, and the guest only spoke Arabic? What if he was covered with piercings and tattoos, or dressed in a peculiar way? How bad would it have to be . . . how many lines would he have to cross before he exceeded the reach of *your* Golden Rule?

One thing is certain—responding to needs at midnight with the heart of a servant creates opportunities later to respond to needs at noontime. And sowing kindness in the darkness, when no one else is looking, will lead to reaping greatly when every eye is awake.

People just want to be treated as people. That's the lesson young James Cash Penney learned at the Golden Rule stores in Wyoming—later to become JCPenney. And that lesson carried him far as a businessman, leader, and entrepreneur, opening more than 1,400 stores by 1929.

Anybody knocking on your door lately?

CHAPTER 2

Explore the Possibilities

I t all started with an idea in the mind of a four-year-old. Cassie certainly wasn't
the first kid to set up shop as a lemonade business. But she'd heard about it or
seen it in a cartoon or something, and she was inspired.

We were living in Birmingham. Corner lot, busy street. But that didn't deter
Miss Entrepreneur and her twin sister. They were out to make some money and
had just discovered a surefire way to do it.

What do you say to a born dreamer with stars in her eyes and a plan for
making her dreams come true?

"Okay."

You say, "Okay."

That's what Mama said, and she went about helping the twins prepare for
their first business venture. Set up a table, make an engaging sign, and of course,
prep a big pitcher of lemonade and cooler of ice.

Then there were the pigtails. I'll never forget the pigtails.

We helped them set up and provided inventory. Their job: sales. Not a problem
though. Who could resist two pigtailed cuties offering a tasty break from the heat?

Apparently everybody. Not one person stopped.

I'll never forget the image of those two hopeful but disappointed girls. As car after
car whizzed by while they baked in the Alabama heat, my heart stirred more and more.

What do you say to a dreamer who has lost the stars in those blue eyes?

"I'm sorry."

You say, "I'm sorry."

And you let them know there'll be a next time.

And a next time there was. This time at Grandmother's house.

Uh, strike two.

The next time was in Fayette, Alabama, after we moved there.

Third time's the . . . third strikeout. Not to worry about Cassie however. She found a way to solve the problem. More on that later.

On that first attempt, as we moved on through our day with our little pig-tailed girls, I made a gut-deep, passionate vow: *as God is my witness, as long as I have breath in my lungs and my hands on the wheel, I will never pass a lemonade stand without stopping.*

I think I can count two occasions where I missed one. On occasions I've taken special trips across town. I've made ridiculous U-turns or gone to the ATM to get some cash, just to buy lemonade from an undersized dreamer. The kids, older now, would groan. Too bad. Robin would sometimes remind me we were in a hurry. Uh huh. Whatever. I had promises to keep.

Through the years I have often wondered why I reacted so strongly to that initial lemonade stand experience. Was it just parental sympathy? I don't think so. I guess in a way I saw myself sitting at that table. Couldn't pull off the pigtail look, but I totally understand the *dream*. When God created us in His image, He gave us the ability to envision something that *isn't* as though it *is*. He created us to be dreamers. Risk takers. Imagination farmers. And that's what this chapter is all about—reconnecting with your capacity to dream. Exploring possibilities limited only by the greatness of your God and the size of your faith.

What If It All Depended on Jesus?
Where Imagination Meets Abundance

Scene 1: Imagine the looks and the laughs. You're a low-wage employee. A social nobody. You own no property, have little to no money. On a busy sidewalk you're nameless and faceless. Yet there you are, in the local real estate office, shopping for investment properties. Or maybe sitting around the local coffee shop, asking about business opportunities. But if anyone knew you, they'd laugh you out the door.

Scene 2. Imagine the awkwardness and anguish. You're a servant. A social nobody. You own no property, have little to no money. On a busy sidewalk . . . well, you get it. Yet there you are, being asked by the most powerful man you know to manage part of his money. More money than you've ever seen, much less ever held in your hand.

Echoes of your parents' proverb still ring in your ear: "A fool and his money are soon parted." Can't he find someone else for the job? This is risky business, and you're no risk taker. Isn't there a hole somewhere?

That's the life of a servant who receives an assignment from God and assumes, "If it's to be, it's up to me." Such thinking can take you in one of two directions. You can swell up like a hotshot or shrink back in fear. But those are actually flip sides of the same coin. *They both mean you're depending on yourself to get the job done.*

Isn't that what you're supposed to do? Doesn't God help those who help themselves?

No. He helps those who are helpless. He helps those who abide in him. He helps those who ask Him to do what only He can do, and who act on His authority.

You can't explore all the possibilities until you start looking through the lens of the source of *all* possibilities. That takes place as the limitless power of Christ flows through His children. Jesus did not come into your life to limit you. He came to empower you, to reflect His goodness, power, and authority. Let's explore the implications of that.

ABIDE IN HIM

Jesus once drew an earthly picture—an allegory—of a heavenly reality. He described himself as a vine, with His Father as the gardener (see John 15:1–11). His followers function as branches. "I am the vine, you are the branches; he who abides in Me and I in him, he bears much fruit, for apart from Me you can do nothing" (John 15:5). As long as we remember our role and our relationships, we will prosper. When we try to be somebody we're not—especially when we try to do God's job—we run into a few problems.

What does it mean to be a branch of the Jesus, the true vine? It means you're made of the same stuff. You receive the life, the nature, and the fruit-bearing power of the vine because you have the vine's nature.

It also means you're dependent. Without Him, you can do nothing. "Nothing" doesn't just refer to "religious things." You can't succeed in *any* endeavor without Him. Not your career, your spiritual life, your family, or anything else.

With Him, however, you can do all things. The possibilities are limitless. This "vine of abundance" is a source of life flowing through you!

Being a branch means you have no capacity to root yourself. All your nourishment comes from the vine. It means that Jesus, the vine, is your faithful source of all you need to fulfill your purpose and potential. Your task is to stay positioned to receive life and power from the vine.

Sometimes we create problems for ourselves by asking the wrong questions. That happens when you make your dreams, yearnings, and struggles a self-centered issue and take your focus off the vine, off Jesus. You find yourself asking questions like, "How can I satisfy the desires of *my* heart? How can I get to the life situation *I* want to be in?"

God's answer: you can't experience the fruitfulness *you* desire apart from abiding in Him. In other words, *it's not about you*—even though you're the dream carrier.

Many of your desires may be quite legitimate. But they don't change the fact that you're a branch, not the vine. There is a difference between the way a branch solves its problems and the way a vine does. In the language of the allegory, your flesh says, "Be the vine, and solve your problems and challenges—as a vine!"

God says, "Do you realize how stupid it is for a branch to act like the gardener?"

In this allegory only one thing is necessary for a branch to satisfy its yearnings or solve problems. It must remain attached to the flow of life from the vine. That is both a warning and a blessing. The blessing is that your life becomes incredibly simplified. Your job is to receive life from Jesus and share it with others. God's job is to figure out how to shape you and where to put you to help you fulfill your purpose.

The warning: stop playing gardener. You're not made for it.

ASK IN HIS NAME

Six times in three chapters (John 14–16), Jesus talks about "asking in His name." Sort of makes me think He's trying to get something across. And He uses some powerful words to go with it: "Ask anything" and "whatever you ask." "You may ask Me for anything in My name," Jesus said, "and I will do it" (John 14:14, NIV). Now either He means that, or He doesn't. James adds that we don't have because we don't ask, or we ask and don't receive because we ask with wrong motives (see James 4:2–3).

So what does it mean to ask in Jesus' name? It means to ask as His representative—to ask as if Jesus was doing the asking. It means asking *for His glory,* out of the overflow of His life abiding in yours.

Christians spend a lot of time pondering unanswered prayers. We get it backward. God is more concerned with *unasked* prayer. It amazes me how after forty-plus years of following Christ, I *still* try every plan and scheme to get something done myself. *Then,* after *everything* else, I hear that tiny whisper: "You haven't asked Me."

Do you want to know if you are abiding—really abiding—in Christ? How's this for evidence? "If you abide in Me, and My words abide in you, ask whatever you wish, and it will be done for you" (John 15:7).

ACT IN HIS AUTHORITY

In the story of the talents, servants were promoted to ambassadors and stewards. Why did the master get so angry with the hoarder? Because he lost a little interest money? Not likely. He was angry because his ambassador reflected poorly on the master's character. He made the master look like a coward.

The miracle of the New Testament age is that the life of the Lord Jesus flows from Him to those who believe in His name. We are no longer just servants of God but ambassadors and friends (see John 15:15; 2 Corinthians 5:20). That means *when God gives you an assignment, He gives the corresponding authority to go with it.*

LifeVestors understand they aren't acting on their own authority. Are you a mother? Be a mother with Jesus' authority. Are you in the professional world? Be a professional in Jesus' name. That doesn't mean the authority to order people around. It means the authority to claim God's resources to do whatever God puts in your heart to do.

Go back to the previous illustration. You're a servant that nobody's ever heard of. But you walk in with power of attorney from your Master, authorizing you to act on His behalf. As you hand the letters to the proper people, you get a completely different response. "Sit right down! Let us show you some of our finest investments."

You walk with a completely different level of confidence. You're courageous enough to take bold action. But you're wise enough to know the source of your power, riches, wisdom, strength, honor, glory, and blessing.

What if it all depended on Jesus? It does. And that's a good thing. But exploring the possibilities also requires us to have the faith and courage to trust God as we forge new territory.

SEED MONEY

1. Read James 4:1–3 and Jeremiah 33:3. If God issued you a free pass to ask anything that would give Him glory, what would you ask for?

2. What are some ways you run into problems because without thinking you try to do God's job for Him? How can you "let go and let God be God"?

3. How would your life change tomorrow if you did everything as a representative of Jesus? How can you act in His authority without acting arrogant or proud?

4. Make a prayer list based on your responses to the first three questions. Set aside time daily this week to talk specifically to the Lord about each of the things on your list.

Leading beyond Your Lifetime
Where Imagination Meets Leadership

It was, without a doubt, one of the lowest periods in my life. I was broke and jobless, living in the wake of my own failures. My whole world had turned upside down. I was torn between two directions. Do I stay in that part of the world I had always considered home? Or venture out to a place I had only seen on trips to my in-laws' house? My wife wanted to be near her parents during that season. I wanted to live in Anywhere Else, USA. "If the world was flat," I said, "Lubbock, Texas, would be on the edge of it."

But my world was flat. Our family divided. Our children scared and hurt. I didn't know what to do. I didn't know anybody in Lubbock. I had no network, no support there. But to be fair to Robin, I had to try. So I made a phone call to my pastor. Did he know anybody? As a matter of fact, yes. As another matter of fact, the man he knew happened to be in Mobile, where I was staying at the time. He owned a business there, my pastor said, and gave me the phone number. He was busy but would be able to squeeze in a few minutes to visit with me about a possible job in Lubbock.

I called. "This is Andy Wood. May I speak to Mister—."

"Oh, you want to speak to Dan," the lady said in a relaxed voice. "He's in a meeting right now, but wanted to know if you could come by at 2:00 today?"

"I'll be there."

I put on my best suit and grabbed a new resume on linen paper. I was a textbook interviewee. But there was no hiding the fact that I needed him far more than he needed me. He was friendly and gracious, but honest. "You're not worth much to me right now," he said, "but I can offer you a job as a sales trainee and provide you with a car." He then offered a salary that was gracious for him, but only about half of my previous job. We never said it, but he and I both knew that in my current distress, I had to keep looking.

But he knew something more. He knew I was living in the land of the walking wounded.

I shook his hand to leave, and he held on to it, looking me in the eye with a gaze that was warm but strong. "If our paths never cross again," he said, "there is something I want you to remember. Don't let people keep score. You know, people love to keep score." Then he repeated his encouragement: "Don't let people keep score."

I needed to hear that. The encouragement helped, far more than he or I realized in that parting moment.

I eventually did move to Lubbock a few months later . . . kicking and screaming, mad at God, my "last act of surrender." That's a story for another time.

I was tooling around town one day on the sprawling campus of Texas Tech University. I saw a sign and did a double take—Dan Law Field, Texas Tech's baseball stadium. The same Dan Law who didn't know me or owe me but had cleared off a spot in his busy schedule to offer me a job. The same Dan Law who, even more important, offered some encouragement. That's what leaders do. It's what LifeVestors do.

"Who *was* that guy?" I asked myself.

Time passed, and with it my good intentions. I often thought about looking up Dan to say, "Thanks for the encouragement on a day I really needed it." I even considered cold-calling him on the phone from time to time but never did.

Five years later I had the privilege of preaching for the first time at Lubbock's First Baptist Church. After the early service, a gracious lady expressed her appreciation for the message.

"I'm Mrs. Dan Law," she said.

I looked at her bug-eyed. "Have you got a minute?" I asked. "I have a story to tell you."

She was delighted to hear it, of course, and told me I'd have my opportunity to say thank you personally in the second service. And thank him I did.

The simplest acts of encouragement, faith, or love can influence people long after your life here is over. But we must be willing to be interrupted or inconvenienced. Dan Law was a successful businessman who understood the power of leaving a legacy. He was also wise enough to know that financial generosity is only one way to do so. To Red Raider baseball, he may have been a benefactor whose name will live on long after his lifetime. But he'll live on in my lifetime as a man who invested in me with his encouragement.

I have long been intrigued with the Bible's testimony of Abel I recounted earlier: "And although Abel is long dead, he still speaks to us by his example of faith"

(Hebrews 11:4, NLT). You too can speak long after you're dead—even without your name on a building. The same book in the Bible that credits Abel's faithful influence gives other examples as well. Those who continue to influence others today through their faith and example.

Abel left a legacy of excellence. He offered God his "firstfruits," the finest of his flocks in worship (see Genesis 4:4). He never said a recorded word, but his willingness to make God his priority and his faith speak volumes. The Lord still testifies of Abel's life to this day.

Enoch left a legacy of intimacy with God (see Genesis 1:25–27). It's no coincidence that his son lived longer than any man in history. Enoch made a lifetime pursuit out of seeking God.

Noah is an example of preparation for the future (see Genesis 6). He was the world's first futurist. First weather forecaster too. He boldly looked into an unprecedented future, with its warning of judgment, and began making choices to prepare himself and his family for it. Boy, does that speak loudly to a generation that often doesn't look past dinnertime.

Abraham's legacy was the example of obedience without guarantees. "By an act of faith, Abraham said yes to God's call to travel to an unknown place that would become his home. When he left he had no idea where he was going" (Hebrews 11:8, MSG). His life still influences those of us who like to have all the results figured out before we decide to act.

Sarah left a legacy of laughter (see Genesis 18, 21). She laughed at the possibilities of having a son in her old age. She wound up laughing at the impossibilities. Laughed so hard, she named her son Laughter. The Hebrew name: Isaac.

Back to Abraham. He left another kind of legacy—sacrifice. "By faith Abraham, when put to the test, offered up Isaac. He who had received the promises was ready to offer up his only son" (Hebrews 11:17, NRSV). Every generation since has felt the influence of a man who was so in love with his God. Abraham did the most God-like thing imaginable—he was willing to sacrifice his only son.

There are more examples, but you get the idea. In the context of leaving a legacy, these people all had two things in common. First, they all were willing to do something no one before them had ever done. They were leaders. They blazed a trail for others to follow. That's the stuff legacies are made of.

Second, they all sacrificed the convenience and comfort of the moment. Each of them had an eye either on the next generation or on eternity. If you want to lead and live on, you'll need to do the same.

Anybody can play it safe. Anybody can look out for Number One. Those who leave a legacy of leadership aren't content to settle for that.

SEED MONEY

1. Read Hebrews 11:1–12. Why do people with great faith live on as examples, while the memory of unbelievers seems to fade away?

2. Sara had her desire for a baby. Abraham had his vision to be the father of a nation. What are you trusting God for? Where are you "living on the edge" or bumping up against the impossible when it comes to faith?

3. Dan Law had encouragement and financial generosity. Noah had carpentry skills. Abel was a man of the firstfruits, and Enoch pursued a walk with God. What do you have to offer that can influence future generations?

4. In response to the questions above, what can you do in the next week that could have a potential influence on tomorrow's child or adult?

What Do You Want?

Where Imagination Meets Increase

How would your life be different if you lived your ideal dream life every day? Where would you live? How would you describe your relationships? How would you spend your time? It's time to give yourself permission to dream. What does "increase" look like to you?

I'm a list maker. You have your quirks; that's mine. Not so much the "to-do" variety—that would make me look more organized than I am. My lists are the more thoughtful type. Let me tell you where it all started.

A few years ago, I was reading a book by Jerrold Mundis about getting out of debt.[1] Somewhere in the middle of it he inserted a simple little chapter on goals. While we were becoming debt-free, it would help to remember why that was important to us in the first place. So he suggested setting goals.

Okay, now you're talkin' my language! I love goals. I've read a lot on goal setting, achievement, success, and vision. The gleam in my eye began to shine in eager anticipation.

Make a list, he said.

That's it?

That was it.

Actually, Mundis suggested three lists. Take three pieces of paper. At the top of one, write, "100 Things I'd Like to Do." Atop the second write, "100 Things I'd Like to Be." On the third, "100 Things I'd Like to Have." Then make your lists. You may not be able to think of 100 things in each category. *No problem,* he said. List what you can.

I was intrigued. I'd never seen anything goal-related expressed so simply. So I took him up on his idea and went to town. I got my three pieces of paper and began to list. I listed both immediate and lifetime goals. He was right! It isn't as easy to think of a hundred things as you may imagine. It was also much easier to list things I wanted to *have* than it was to list things I wanted to *be*.

Over the next couple of months, I spent hours on my lists and enjoyed every minute. I relished thinking, dreaming, reflecting. I was whimsical with some, deadly serious with others. I enjoyed putting "the respect of my children" on the same *have* list as "a new putter." I made no value judgments on the list until later. I just wrote.

I learned a lot about myself from my lists. I rediscovered what my values were, for better or worse. I learned how important it was for me make a difference in other people's lives. I also awoke the deep desire I have for personal freedom and intellectual growth. I realized how contradictory some of my priorities can be.

I also discovered the power of simply listing what I want. Some things began to happen because I'd written them down. Others required a sequence of steps or an enormous amount of discipline. I've experienced the fulfillment of some and said, "So what? Now what?" Others provided priceless, lifelong memories. Many of the things I listed that I wanted have yet to be realized.

What do you want? More money? Not very spiritual, but it beats the alternative. More love? A deeper connection with certain people? A second chance to visit the site of your honeymoon? To play that special golf course or float the Colorado River?

What about the intangibles? How about the respect of your children? Or to be a positive spiritual influence on someone in particular? What about the restoration of a severed relationship? All those and more are on my lists. Why not make some lists of your own?

But what good is a list of wishes without a course that lays out how to experience them? Let's look at what Jesus had to say about going from wishes to fulfillment. You'll find it by asking, acting, and giving.

ASK

Let's not overlook the obvious. God established His kingdom so things happen as a result of the praying of His people. I love the way the Message paraphrases the words of Jesus: "Don't bargain with God. Be direct. Ask for what you need. This isn't a cat-and-mouse, hide-and-seek game we're in" (Matthew 7:7, MSG).

Think about this. *Your life today is the direct result of what you've asked God to make it and what you believed it would become.* Are there exceptions to that? Of course. But I've observed that when I experience a Day from Hell, it's often because I didn't ask God for anything different. Or I asked with no faith or with selfish motives.

What do you want? Ask God for it and be specific. He says, "Call to Me, and I will answer you, and show you great and mighty things, which you do not know" (Jeremiah 33:3, NKJV).

He eagerly awaits a chance to show you how powerful and faithful He can be with the desires of your heart. Does that mean He's a celestial Santa Claus? No. He's not a cosmic killjoy either. Pray big; God will answer big. Pray specifically; God will answer specifically. "You do not have because you do not ask" (James 4:2, NASB).

I should also point out here that when Jesus says, "Ask," He doesn't limit receiving to asking God for it. Sometimes, besides asking God directly, He calls us to ask *somebody else*. Try it! Discover the power of bold asking.

ACT

Sometimes we're praying when God has other ideas. Sometimes He wants us to be the answer to our own prayer—or somebody else's. I once heard of a dad who was leading a family prayer time. He told God about the many needs of the poor widow across the street. Tears of sympathy rolled down his wife's cheeks. But one member of the family wasn't praying. He was thinking. When Dad said, "Amen," his son walked over to him with his hand held out. "Dad," he said, "give me your wallet and I'll go over there and answer your prayer myself."

Sometimes when we ask the Lord to do something, He says, "No! *You* do it!" *You* make the call. *You* show the love. *You* touch the heart. *You* serve the meal. *You* clean up the mess. *You* ask for the job. He doesn't send you and abandon you, but He does send you. That's especially true when it's related to one of your goals or dreams. *Nobody* is more committed to your fulfillment than you are. The Lord will empower you, embolden you, and wise you up. People will give you more help and support than you deserve. But sooner or later, you'll have to actually *do* something.

GIVE

> *"Give away your life; you'll find life given back, but not merely given back—given back with bonus and blessing. Giving, not getting, is the way. Generosity begets generosity"*
>
> Luke 6:38, MSG

That's a universal principle, applicable to any dimension of life. It's also tridirectional. When my son, Joel, first introduced me to the idea of LifeVesting, he talked about three levels: GodVesting, OtherVesting, and SelfVesting. The return Jesus talked about will come from the same three places we invest. As you give to God, God will return to you, "with bonus and blessing." As you give to others,

others will give back. As you invest in yourself, you increase your capacity to receive as well as give more in the future.

Let's put it all together. Suppose your life's dream is to be a physician. So you *ask*. "Oh, God, make me a doctor." He's perfectly capable of doing that. Most likely though, He'll say, "*Act!* Go to medical school." You take the tests (*asking* for God's mercy and help), and you're in. You *give* of your time and money to invest in yourself and the future care of your patients. You're now past asking; you're *begging* God for help. And every day you *act* in the direction of your dream. In the process you *give* your services and instruction to others who need care and learning as well. It's a marvelous process. And it requires the continuous interchange of asking, acting, and giving.

So what *do* you want?

SEED MONEY

1. "He eagerly awaits a chance to show you how powerful and faithful He can be with the desires of your heart." What is a recent example of answered prayer that you have experienced? How does it reflect your understanding of God's heart?

2. Read James 1:19–27. Do you have a gap between being a hearer and being a doer of God's instructions? What are some areas in your life where the practicing needs to catch up with the preaching or the hearing?

3. How important is the help of others to you? Are you more of a groupie or a loner? Do you depend completely on others, try to fly solo on every dream, or somewhere in-between? Why?

4. Try it yourself. Make a list. If you want, make three—a *do,* a *be,* and a *have* list. If not those, make one of your own choosing. But start documenting your desires and goals.

The Clarifying Question
Where Imagination Meets Freedom

"I need to talk to you about your lab results."

(My doctor.)

I was sure it was the usual—cholesterol, triglycerides, blah, blah.

"No, it's your blood sugar."

"Oh, well I had some cereal the night before . . . "

Sorry, Charlie. Not what he was talking about. I wasn't excusing myself out of this one. Dr. Gage introduced me to something called A1C. "What this means is you are a Type-2 diabetic."

You can talk to your doctor about the medical side of all that. Let me apply a LifeVesting lens to what I heard. *Andy, you've been a sugar consumer for years. Now the choices you have made in your diet and lack of exercise have left you in bondage. You used up today's insulin yesterday. Now today it's payback time. You chose poorly yesterday. You're in debt today.*

Exploring the possibilities isn't just a happy mental trip to Dreamland. It also means taking a sober look at possible results of your choices. The freedom—and bondage—you experience today are the results of decisions you made yesterday. Owning your future involves exploring the results of your decisions before you make them. You probably do that already with your major decisions. But what about those thoughtless lifestyle choices? What about your habits? What about your word choices or use of time? What about that late-night bowl of cereal?

This doesn't have to be complicated or drawn-out. You can ask yourself a simple but profound question to give you instant clarity. Did I choose well? You'll live well. Or did I choose poorly? You'll serve the consequences of those choices too.

Moses understood that. Just before his death, he called an assembly of Israelites for one last talk. There he reframed all the things God had taught them. We call it Deuteronomy. Here's what Moses had to say as he was wrapping things up:

> *"This day I call the heavens and the earth as witnesses against you*
> *that I have set before you life and death, blessings and curses. Now choose*
> *life, so that you and your children may live."*
>
> Deuteronomy 30:19, NIV

There's one example of a clarifying question: *am I choosing life or death?* A friend of mine started using this to frame his everyday decisions. That includes what he eats, his business decisions, and his family relationships.

Jesus offered another way to frame your choices. "Take care!" He said. "Don't do your good deeds publicly, to be admired, for then you will lose the reward from your Father in heaven" (Matthew 6:1, TLB). Based on that you could ask, *When and where do I want the benefits of this choice?* Here or there? Today or eternity? My pleasure or God's?

Wise choices today will provide the freedom to have more choices available in the future. That's the LifeVesting principle of freedom. In that context try this clarifying question: *in the future, will this decision free me or bind me?*

I'm pausing a minute here while you let that sink in.

Some choices bind you in the future. They leave you enslaved to the consequences or addicted to the choice itself. Other choices serve you instead. They create possibilities that free you to fulfill your potential.

Want a great case study in living with the results of choices? Check out the life of David, the giant-killing shepherd-king. He made some stupid choices and served those decisions for the rest of his days. But that doesn't tell the complete story of David's life. From his earliest years, he also made choices that ended up serving him. Choices about excellence, courage, principle, and worship. Choices to stand and fight when the entire army of Israel turned and ran. Choices not to retaliate when Saul or Absalom tried to kill him. All these and more led to the testimony from God Himself that David was "a man after His own heart" (1 Samuel 13:14).

In the Sermon on the Mount, Jesus talked about choices that serve us in the future (see Matthew 6:1–18). He defines what it takes to produce a future reward by reducing it to three simple things:

Do the right thing,
with the right attitude,
for the right reason.

ACTION: DO THE RIGHT THING

Jesus spoke of three types of action—giving, praying, and fasting—that produce a future return. These actions represent three broader themes. Everything you do in the name of godliness will fall into one of these three categories:

- Meeting the needs of others
- Developing intimacy with God
- Self-discipline

LifeVestors are generous. They give. When? When somebody has a need. They don't judge, whine, preach, manipulate, or wait till the cameras are rolling. They find a need and serve it. If they don't have the resources themselves, they help find them, if they can. They don't do it to be noticed. They aren't martyrs about it either. They know they can't meet every need, but they serve the needs they can.

LifeVestors pursue intimacy, especially with God. They recognize that prayer isn't often urgent but is always important. And LifeVestors pursue the important with quietness, intensity, honesty, and consistency. As they pursue the heart of their heavenly Father, they learn to forgive and be forgiven (see Matthew 6:14–15). As a result they experience intimacy with others as well.

LifeVestors discipline themselves. As with fasting, they see the value of doing without today, so they can harness greater power tomorrow. Yes, they do it with food. They also do it with time, energy, entertainment, and money. Paul understood that. That's why he encouraged Timothy to "exercise yourself toward godliness" (1 Timothy 4:7, NKJV).

ATTITUDE: THE CHECKUP FROM THE NECK UP

How you do things is as important sometimes as what you do. You can do everything right on the outside but ruin the results with a sour or selfish attitude.

Jesus warned against three self-serving attitudes. They were easy to spot in the religious leaders of His day. The first is pride—doing what you do to be noticed and praised. The second is pretense—trying to create an impression about yourself that isn't true. The third is false misery—trying to arouse sympathy from others by your huge sacrifices.

There's a common thread in all these. A life-consumer invests in impression management. That's like taking your whole life's earnings and buying the biggest fireworks display of all time. People may be amazed and impressed—today. Tomorrow they'll just look for someone who can top what you did. And they *will* find it. Meanwhile you've pulled your trigger. You had your reward.

LifeVestors display different attitudes. They love people unselfishly but don't live to please them. They're humble enough to recognize that tomorrow they may need the help. They live and relate to others with simplicity. They recognize the value of simple answers and straight talk. They're filled with praise and wonder and stay submitted to and dependent on God. They value unity and togetherness; they're quick to forgive and seek forgiveness. Through it all, they maintain a steadfast, almost stubborn, spirit of joy. In the end these attitudes are returned to them—often when they need it most.

MOTIVES: DOING IT FOR THE RIGHT REASON

Motives are the invisible movers of the heart. They're known only to God. You can't accurately judge someone else's motives, and your own can be hard to discern as well. That's why God says,

> *"The heart is more deceitful than all else*
> *And is desperately sick;*
> *Who can understand it?*
> *I, the LORD, search the heart,*
> *I test the mind."*

Jeremiah 17:9–10

God tests not just *what* you did but *why*. Your intentions and goals matter. It's possible to do the right thing, even with the right attitude, but with the wrong motives. That's why it's critical to pray, like David:

> *Search me, O God, and know my heart;*
> *test my thoughts. Point out anything you find in me that makes you*
> *sad, and lead me along the path of everlasting life.*

Psalm 139:23–24, TLB

I'm happy to report that as I write this, I've taken charge of my health choices. I don't serve sugar anymore; it serves me. And I feel wonderfully free.

Find a way to keep the clarifying question in front of you. *Will this decision free me or bind me?* Invest in your own freedom by asking the question before you make decisions. Do it consistently; you'll make better choices. And those choices *will* serve you in the future.

And now for some possibilities that will serve you even longer But first . . .

SEED MONEY

1. Write about an example of a choice you made when you "wound up bound up" afterward. How about a choice that wound up serving you?

2. How's your attitude lately? What's good and what needs adjusting? How is the Holy Spirit alerting you to the need for change or for new steps of obedience?

3. Read Matthew 6:1–18. What insights do you find about *God's* motives, attitudes, and behavior?

4. What is one correction you can make or action you can take that will move you toward greater freedom?

Here Comes the Neighbor-hood
Where Imagination Meets Eternity

What would you do if you were Jimmy? You're caught in a dilemma because your best friend is a hood. Riffraff. Wrong side of the tracks. Your parents say you can't visit him. And he'd do as well to stay on his side of town too. But there's something special about him; that's why he's your best friend. He doesn't have much, but he does have heart and passion.

And a cheap, second-hand guitar he doesn't even know how to tune.

You come from a good family with something of a pedigree. You live in one of the music capitals of America, and your cousin is a famous country musician. Maybe you can still be his friend, this kid some people call "white trash."

Maybe you can introduce your friend to your cousin and he can cross the tracks in your place.

That's what Jimmy did. He asked his cousin to meet with the boy, and the cousin agreed. There on a back lane near his house, the singer showed the dreamer how to tune his instrument and play a few basic chords. It wasn't much, but the kid wasn't looking for much. Just an opportunity, a chance.

What *did* you do if you were Jimmy? And you introduced your cousin to the best friend your parents forbade you to visit?

You played a role—a bit part—in the transformation of a culture.

You made a difference in the life of Elvis Presley.

It's one thing to make a sale or impact an organization. It's another to touch someone else in such a way that your influence lives for all eternity. You have plenty of possibilities in front of you to do just that. But be advised—many of those opportunities come cleverly disguised.

WHAT IF *YOU* WERE THE HOOD?

Shift gears a minute. What if you were Jimmy—and *you* were the hood? What if you were minding your own business on your side of the tracks and found your friend's parents—mugged? Robbed. Bloody and unconscious. For all you know, they could blame you. God knows, they've blamed plenty else on you.

This is your moment of opportunity.

What would you do?

Did I mention they are racists, and you're, well, a race?

What would you do now?

Did I mention if they weren't beaten unconscious and left for dead, they'd as soon die as take help from you?

How about now?

Want a little more drama? What if I were to tell you there's a pretty good like-lihood that the muggers are still in the 'hood, watching you? Or that the cops are on the way, and if they catch you kneeling in that pool of blood, you'll do the time?

Come on, Jimbo. Walk away. If your friend's parents were conscious, they'd say the same thing. You don't owe them anything.

Except to love them (see Romans 13:8).

To invest in them.

To introduce them to Somebody you know who can help them.

What we have here is an opportunity, disguised as danger, wrapped in a dilemma. And it's a far more common experience than you may realize.

WHERE TO FIND YOUR INVESTMENTS

Being a LifeVestor means learning to spot opportunities. I once heard of a sculp-tor who created a unique humanlike figure called "Opportunity." The artist had chiseled a covering of hair where the statue's face would have been and crafted wings on both his feet. He explained that its face was hidden because we seldom know Opportunity when he comes to us. The wings on both feet represented the sad truth that Opportunity is soon gone. And once gone, he cannot be overtaken.

The worst time to talk about opportunities is *after* they happen. The prob-lem is, many of our opportunities come disguised as something else. I wonder how many chances you've encountered lately that came disguised as problems. Or people. Or difficult decisions. Or disappointments. Or delays. Or disease. How many of those opportunities did you seize?

"But I don't have many opportunities," you say, "only obstacles." Did it ever occur to you that opportunities and obstacles are two sides of the same coin? As that coin turns, sometimes the opportunity lands faceup; sometimes the obstacle does. But rarely do you encounter one without the other. Every opportunity has its obstacles. Every obstacle has an opportunity sitting close by.

Go back to that thinly veiled modernization of the Good Samaritan story (see Luke 10:25–37). You may want to reread the account. It's filled with clues about where you can find opportunities to invest—not only in your future but in eternity. But to find them, you'll have to look where even the religious pros don't notice, or don't care.

Start with one of my favorites—*interruptions*. The priest and the Levite in Jesus' story no doubt had good reasons for not stopping. But so did the Samaritan. He had a family too. He was busy too. No doubt a little afraid too. But he was willing to be interrupted—to have his own agenda suspended for a greater need or opportunity.

Think about the last time somebody interrupted you to the point of annoying. Where might you have found an opportunity to do more than fuss or fume? How might you have invested rather than hoarded your time and attention?

The *needs of others*. There you'll find opportunities galore. Born out of compassion (which means "to suffer with"), the Samaritan did what was necessary to heal the stranger's pain. In this case it was a physical wound. But sometimes LifeVestors heal emotional or spiritual wounds. Sometimes they act or speak up for those who have no voice of their own, who have suffered injustice. Sometimes they simply meet needs, however servile or unbecoming the task may appear.

Those whining little kids of yours? When they learn they can bring you their little troubles today, they'll trust you later with the big stuff. Believe me, nobody thinks it's glamorous to clean up someone else's vomit, or comfort their broken heart. But you'll find opportunities anywhere you find a need. And as you serve the need, you'll have the opportunity to introduce people to your famous Relative. And I'm not talking about a country musician.

Did I mention the ultimate opportunity to touch a life? Did I mention *forgiveness*? We've whitewashed the word *Samaritan* today. In the first century people said it through their teeth. To be Samaritan was to be hated by any self-respecting Jew. You were a half-breed—a nobody at best, loathed and despised at worst. You were a first-century hood. So you learned from birth to hate back. To invent your own religion, theology, morality, and sense out of life. Who needed Jews anyway?

But what happens when the people who have hurt you are now hurt themselves? Doesn't it serve them right? Aren't they getting something they somehow deserve? Doesn't God want somebody else to help them? Somebody with the same skin color, pedigree, theology, or language? Somebody who actually likes them?

No. He wants you. Hurt feelings, wounded pride, and all. He wants *you* to bridge the gap, to meet the need, to give the money, to finish the job. Not for somebody who *deserves* it, but precisely because they *don't* deserve it. Otherwise it wouldn't be forgiveness.

WHERE'S YOUR FOCUS?

Some people only see the obstacles. Like the children of Israel on the edge of Canaan, they live as though God has only told them part of the story. They've been burned, disappointed, or lied to by the world one time too many. They can see a rainbow and be sure it's raining somewhere. They don't need the devil, the world, or even the Lord to make them miserable. They've already done a pretty good job of it themselves.

Others only see the opportunities. These likable but naive folks would charge hell armed only with a water pistol and a smile. They're often unprepared for the battle or disappointments that lie ahead. And the results can be devastating.

There's another way. Here's how Paul approached it:

> *A wide door for effective service has opened to me, and there are many adversaries.*
>
> 1 Corinthians 16:9

Paul saw both the opportunities and the adversaries. Soberly but faithfully. Decisiveness guided by alertness. You can do the same.

Keep your eyes open. Really open. The opportunities are everywhere. And the results can last forever. But those chances don't stay around long. In the meantime—never, never, never pass by a kid-run lemonade stand. Whatever has you so busy, unless it's life-threatening, just isn't that important.

SEED MONEY

1. Read John 4:1–38. How did Jesus recognize, respond, and teach about opportunities to reach out to people?

2. What if you could bring back a missed opportunity to share your faith or show love to someone? Which chance would you do over? How would you respond differently? How might the results change?

3. What opportunities do you see in your current problems or challenges? Conversely, how about your opportunities—do you see potential pitfalls there?

4. Opportunities call for action! What one action step will you make this week to respond to the opportunities in front of you?

FINAL THOUGHT

Back to the lemonade seller. I mentioned that Cassie solved the problem after strike three. Here's what she and Kate, her neighborhood friend, did. Once they figured out that nobody was going to stop, they took a stack of Styrofoam cups and a pitcher of room temperature beverage and went door-to-door.

"Wanna buy some lemonade?" they asked, smiling.

They sold out.

I'll let you figure out those life lessons yourself.

CHAPTER 3

Follow Your Passion

You've never heard of Yarbo. Unless, of course, you've driven through Washington County, Alabama. This unincorporated community on Highway 17 flies by your car window pretty fast. A couple of old chicken houses, an abandoned softball field, a few house trailers—that's about it.

At least that's how it looks through my window. Yarbo is a place on the way to some other place.

My dad had a different view.

On his trips from Millry to Chatom, he'd see a singular figure sitting in the shade of a mobile home. An older black gentleman spent hours there, offering a friendly wave at passersby. And there in the warmth of those southwest Alabama summer days, my father found a kindred spirit.

He waved back.

Eventually he began to look for his nameless friend as he drove by and made a point of tooting his horn and waving. Though separated by so much culture, each man found a point of connection in a simple gesture.

That wasn't enough for my dad. One day his curiosity got the best of him.

Who was this man? What was his story?

So Daddy did what Daddy did. He stopped and asked. He got his highway friend's name. What he did for a living. His family. What he'd done since retirement.

That unelected mayor and ambassador of Yarbo passed away a few years ago. But my dad never tired of telling the story.

A businessperson may refer to that as networking. A journalist may call it investigative reporting. A pastor or deacon or Sunday school teacher may refer to it as showing the love of Christ. An anthropologist may see it as reaching across a social or cultural divide.

To my dad it was just life. The relentless pursuit of relationships was as normal as breathing.

It was his *passion*.

AN UNSPOKEN AGREEMENT

We were different in so many ways. Ever the extrovert, it was Daddy who would typically make the calls. And like any phone call to somebody who stays busy, those calls were an interruption in my day. But our unspoken agreement was simple. When he called, I answered. His calls to me, though they may have interrupted, were important.

During certain times and seasons, the phone wouldn't ring for a couple of days. Then I would call him to see what the heck was the matter. Usually he'd be off gallivanting on one of his travels, doing extended work in the yard, or hanging out with friends.

THE RULES ARE PRETTY SIMPLE SS

The operative word here is *relentless*. My dad knew no strangers. He never saw a reason to be standoffish or unfriendly. He also was no age snob. He was just as at home with an infant or toddler as he was with a fellow senior or somebody in-between.

In the relentless pursuit of relationships, the rules are simple. When in doubt, move *toward* people, not away from them. You walk in the door. You make the call.

When my father wondered what I was up to, he didn't just sit there and guess, and he *certainly* didn't assume I was busy. He walked in the door. He made the call.

When I was on a stage or behind a pulpit for some significant event, he didn't just celebrate in proud silence. He walked in the door. He made the call.

When I disappointed him, or my life was a broken-down mess, he didn't sulk or hide out in embarrassed silence. He walked in the door. He made the call.

When our kids or grandkids were born, he didn't allow the miles between us to form barriers. He walked in the door. He made the call.

When it became obvious that he and I were very different, he didn't allow our differences to forge a division. Time and time again he walked in the door. He made the call. The relentless pursuit of relationships was my dad's passion—his driving force.

How to Find Your Driving Force

Where Passion Meets Abundance

Remember when you wanted that whatever-it-was from Santa Claus? Or your employer? Or your spouse or parents or educators or whoever . . . only to get it and be disappointed?

Remember when you thought, "If I could just make *this* amount of money, I would be content"? And you did . . . and you weren't.

Remember the time you dreamed and dreamed about a huge desire and were disappointed? But it didn't keep you from dreaming some more.

Remember when you didn't have your health, or didn't have any money, or didn't have any*body*, and it was all you could think about? Then when health or wealth or some*body* showed up, it only served to point out something else you didn't have. And then all you think about was *that*.

We all have something inside that stirs us, motivates us, alarms us, or moves us in certain directions. But that same thing never quite allows us to rest once we get where we were headed or what we desired.

Behind all your choices, actions, reactions, and obsessions lies a hidden mover. It defines your happiness, drives your decisions, and gives you the will to keep doing what you're doing.

I'm talking about your *driving force,* and yes, you have one. You may have more than one.

Your driving force is the "passion behind your passion." It's your dream maker, your prime mover. In the poetic sense, it's what gets you out of bed in the morning. (Unless your driving force *is* the bed; then you have some real problems.)

Your driving force is often the answer to questions like:

- Why did you react like that?
- Why can't you get that off your mind?
- Why don't you just quit?

It goes by other names. My favorite is *treasure*. As in "where your treasure is, there your heart will be also" (Matthew 6:21).

Your driving force makes you uncomfortable where you are. Restless. Even a bit unhappy until you pursue whatever direction it is leading you. But here's where it gets tricky. We don't always *know* what that direction is. Or what our driving force is. We just know it's, well, *driving*.

So sometimes we get it wrong. And getting it wrong can be costly, if not disastrous. You can lose a lot of time, money, and relationships chasing something you *think* is your driving force. That can be devastating if you discover too late you were wrong.

Raise your hand if you're thinking something like this right now: "Hmphh. My driving force is Jesus."

Maybe your driving force is Jesus and maybe it isn't. Or maybe it's a mixed bag. The big question is, *how can you know?* How can you keep from being deceived?

Here are six ways you can trace your treasure:

1. CHECK YOUR CHECKBOOK.

Your driving force may not *be* money, but it sure controls your finances. That explains why a guy with an arsenal in his den, bedroom, and closet just *has* to buy that new rifle. Or why if your power gets cut off, you'll stop what you're doing and fix the problem any way you can.

You don't have unlimited money. So over the long haul, you'll spend what you have on what matters most to you. That also explains why you *don't* spend money in certain situations.

Go ahead and try to pretend your situation is different if you want to. But no less than Jesus Christ Himself said your heart and treasure were linked.

2. LISTEN TO WHAT YOU SAY.

Jesus again: "Out of the abundance of the heart the mouth speaks" (Matthew 12:34, NKJV). Know why you're willing to bore people to tears with tales of gardening, grandchildren, or fishing? They're important to you. That's also why people criticize, joke, preach, encourage, and whine. They're declaring the contents of their hearts. Out of the abundance of the heart people tell stories.

They express love, take God's name in vain, or yell at people that can't hear them in traffic.

If you're brave, have someone secretly record your conversations at various points throughout the day. Watch for patterns. Listen for the driving force.

3. THINK ABOUT YOUR THOUGHTS.

What do you wish for? Plan for? Obsess over? Who do you miss? Despise? Vow to avenge? Who or what fascinates you? Frightens you? Look for shadows of the driving force there.

Paul told the Philippians that every time he thought of them he thanked his God. He also gushed that he couldn't wait to see them again (see Philippians 1:3, 5). That's the language of the driving force.

When David said he thirsted for God like a "deer pants for the water brooks" (Psalm 42:1, NKJV), that's also driving-force language.

Your treasure controls or the thoughts of your heart and mind. What occupies your thinking? It could be a problem to solve, a relationship to heal, a dream to fulfill, or a debt to pay. The fact that you dwell on it says something about your driving force.

4. ANALYZE WHAT OCCUPIES YOUR TIME.

In Ephesians 5:16, Paul warns us to be careful how we live, "redeeming the time, because the days are evil" (NKJV). You and I have different amounts of money or talent. But we have the same time budget. And how you spend your time reflects the driving force of your heart. When you say, "I don't have time," you're saying, "This isn't important to me." But working, waiting, meeting, and connecting are all expressions of commitment and priority.

Yes, it's quite possible that video games matter more than family or friends. Or that social media is more important than social connections. Or work success is more important than marriage success. It's all about the driving force.

5. HEED WHAT YOU HOLD ON TO.

Jesus once compared the kingdom of heaven to a treasure (there's that word again) hidden in a field. When a man finds it, he hides the treasure, and for the sheer joy of it, sells everything and buys the field (see Matthew 13:44). The treasure hunter wouldn't give up that find for anything. Why? The driving force in him valued the treasure.

How about you? What makes you defensive or protective? What do you refuse to give up? What or who do you cling to even while giving up other important things or people? You'll find the driving force there on some scale. It may be small-scale (picture my coffee in the morning) or the level of a life calling. Doesn't matter. When Jacob said to the angel, "I will not let you go until you bless me," and his wife said to Jacob, "Give me children or I die!" that is gut-level driving-force material.

6. EXAMINE YOUR EMOTIONS.

Your feelings are a big clue—especially the ones so strong they surprise you. Your driving force will use emotions more than any other natural source to move you to action. Pay attention to anger, desire, joy, tears, and excitement. Those are the most common handles your driving force will use to spur you on.

You get excited about the things you treasure. You weep over the things you treasure. If something doesn't affect you emotionally, chances are you don't love it very much.

I can't stress enough the importance of knowing your driving force. Do a little soul-searching. You may discover that the force driving you is healthier and more powerful than you thought. Or you may discover that your driving force(s) is selfish, powerless, or ungodly. If so, I have good news: if you don't like your driving force, you can always change it. I know, that sounds contradictory to everything I've said about your driving force thus far. But here's one of the most important

LifeVesting secrets: your life is driven by often-invisible passions—but *you are not bound to them*. You can take control over who or what's currently controlling or driving you.

Meanwhile, as we explore in the next section, nowhere is passion more revealed than when we contemplate our mortality. And that always leads us to face three things—what we believe, how we face an uncertain future, and who or what we cherish most. Those three things—faith, hope, and love—turn our driving force into thousands of points of influence. And when it's time to change that driving force, faith, hope, and love point the way. By reprogramming your faith, refocusing your hope, and redirecting your love, you bring your driving force into alignment with God's highest and best for your life. More on that later in this chapter.

SEED MONEY

1. Read the first chapter of Philippians. List the different ways Paul revealed his driving force(s) in that chapter. What was he passionate about?

2. Take an inventory of where your money goes over the course of a month, quarter, or year. What does that tell you about your top priorities?

3. Describe a time when you were surprised by how forcefully you reacted to a situation. Thinking about that experience now, what does that tell you about your driving force?

4. "If you don't like your driving force, you can always change it." What have you discovered about your driving force that needs a change? What specific steps can you take to make that change?

Three Things (Always) Remain
Where Passion Meets Leadership

Write your epitaph. That was the assignment. I was attending a goal-setting semi-nar sponsored by a local business. We were completing a series of exercises to help us clarify our highest priorities.

But this was no press release or publicity sheet. I had to assume the ulti-mate—I'm dead. All that's left of me is what I could stuff into this vapor of a life. So, supposing I had some control over how I would be remembered, what was Andy known for?

Up until this time in the seminar, I'd enjoyed visions of success. Suddenly I was face-to-face with significance. It was moving. Sobering. Eye-opening. They gave us fifteen minutes; I was done in five. I was surprised how quickly the words flowed on paper. And to this day they remain in my prayer notebook just as I wrote them.

Andy Wood was known for:

Making a difference in the lives of others, beginning with his own.
A faithful husband, loving father, a man of God, and a man of integrity.
A man who was a builder, first of human lives, then of more tangible things.
A man who knew how to laugh, especially when others were sad or miserable.
A man who knew adversity and overcame it.
One who bred loyalty in people.
One who loved to create.
Who understood and fulfilled his life purpose, and who helped others find theirs.
And one who remained throughout his life a friend of children.

What was so eye-opening about that? The fact that it was less about achieve-ment and more about relationships. Less about my estate and more about the effect I had on others. And stripped of pleasure, profit, and power, I realized what matters most to me is faith, hope, and love.

How do I know that I've made a difference in the lives of others? When they believe more, hope more, love more.

How do I know I was a faithful husband, loving father, and a man of God? When those who know me best are encouraged and equipped to believe more, hope more, love more.

How do I know if I was a builder of human lives? When the humans I helped build believe more, hope more, love more.

That's the stuff of passion.

That's the stuff of leadership.

"Three things will last forever, Paul said, "faith, hope, and love—and the greatest of these is love" (1 Corinthians 13:13, NLT). What you really believe. What you confidently expect from the future. Who you really love. Even if there were no heaven or eternal life, those three factors form the key to your future influence.

FAITH: WHAT'S YOUR BS?

An old saying in faith circles states, "What you believe is what you live. All the rest is just religious talk." Amen! Furthermore, what you believe and live will be passed on to a new generation. They may accept it or reject it, but they'll certainly inherit it. That's one of the miracles of biblical Christianity. It's always one generation away from extinction, yet the kingdom will live forever from one generation to the next (see Daniel 2:44).

A few years ago I started keeping a list of my BS—my belief system. I started taking a hard look at how I lived and what others were picking up from me. I wanted to think through what motivated me to be excited or angry. I started with my orthodox beliefs about God and the Bible but moved past that. The result is a list of pithy little things that mean nothing to anybody else but me. Things like, "The measure of the server is in the refills of the tea." Or "Respect is measured by your willingness to listen." What's interesting, though, is how I've seen some of those beliefs replicated in my wife, children, and others.

So how about you? What's your BS? What will it say to your pallbearers? How will it continue to speak, long after your voice is silent? What will it say about reality, virtue, priorities, or Jesus? Your faith will live longer than you do. You pass it along every day. Not the faith you *talk* but the faith you *walk*.

HOPE: DON'T STOP THINKING ABOUT TOMORROW

It was the first contradiction between parent and teacher in my daughter's life. Carrie was a little freaked out about some impending disaster her teacher reported as fact during the science lesson that day. Riding in the car, she asked me in first-grade language what I thought about the certain doom of our planet. I found myself speaking from the depths of my soul—using words I'd never put together in the same sentence before. "Carrie," I said from my gut, *"never, never, never* believe anyone who would make you afraid of the future."

(I liked the sound of that so much, I went home and added it to my BS list!)

You will impact generations by the way you approach the future. Lillian Hearst understood that. Lillian lived to be ninety-two years old, and I was privileged to be her pastor. Just after her death I learned that she always had something planned to do the next day—something to anticipate, something to prepare for, a reason to get out of bed in the morning. It sounds simple, but it struck me as profound. Maybe that's one of the reasons she lived so long. Lillian had hope, and hope is contagious.

Life is filled with uncertainties, so people constantly seek whatever can build their confidence to face them. When you find your hope, others will follow to the degree that you grip it with confidence. They won't be fooled by your wishful words. But they'll tend to find future confidence in the same things or people you do.

Jesus was and is the ultimate hope dealer. He had a way of showing up at the most hopeless moments and infusing them with new possibilities. He wasn't insensitive or blind to the pain of others. He even wept at Lazarus's tomb, knowing He was going to raise Lazarus from the dead. But in dealing with problems or pain, Jesus never accepted them as the final word. Neither should you. LifeVestors don't pretend problems don't exist, but they do hold on to the hope that problems can and will be solved.

LOVE: ONE THING STANDS OUT

Love stands taller, Paul said. It reaches further. Lives longer. Wanna guarantee the death of your influence, even before you die? Live without loving. Invest only in yourself. Hold on to that resentment. Become an eternal victim. Argue, at length, with anybody who disagrees with you. Break your promises to your family. Quit when the relationship starts getting gritty. Demand that everybody else in your world serves you because you're entitled to it. Become jealous anytime somebody else gets praise or recognition. Criticize often. Complain even more. Never trust anybody. Get even. You'll be in good company, though you probably won't like the neighbors.

Love is that place where passion meets life-long influence. Here's one more thought from scripture:

> *Our teaching about this journey is intended to bring us to a single destination—a place where self-giving love reigns from a pure heart, a clean conscience, and a genuine faith.*
>
> 1 Timothy 1:5, VOICE

Three things remain. Three things *always* remain. How would the people who know you best describe your faith, hope, and love? What do you want your faith, hope, and love to say to future generations about you? Or about Jesus? What can you do today to believe more, hope more, or love more?

Here's a hint: get in touch with your deepest, God-given desires. More on that in the next section.

SEED MONEY

1. Read 1 Corinthians 13:4–7. Rewrite it, substituting your name for "love" and giving an example of how that may be true. Example: "Andy is patient. He never gets irritated when he's interrupted or has to repeat a sentence or an action."

2. What does your future look like to you today? Describe tomorrow, or this time next year or ten years from now if your life keeps moving in the same direction it is right now.

3. Start your own BS (Belief System) list. What do you believe about love, life, people, priorities, absurdities? How do your beliefs affect your life for better or for worse?

4. Based on your answers to the previous three questions, what is the most impactful change you can make in either your love, your expectations of the future (your hope), or your beliefs?

Investing in Your Deepest Longings
Where Passion Meets Increase

Today it seems little. Important, yes, but on a miniature scale. But on that day, it was larger than life—even larger than health. A life-changing lesson awaited.

From the time I was fifteen years old, I knew God was leading me to be a pastor. I also knew the pathway to get there, and five years later I was still on that path, about to graduate from college. For a year I'd been serving at my first church, full-time in the summer and on the weekends during school. The people there were gracious and patient. It had been a wonderful experience. Now, as I was about to graduate, both the church and I were preparing to move on.

Because I had blown through college in three years, I decided to lay out a year before going to graduate school. When the church caught wind of it, they were delighted to offer me a full-time position. They offered me more than twice what I had ever made in a year. I said it sounded good, but let me take the week and pray about it, and I'd let them know the next Sunday. I left town that night assuming the next year of my life was set.

One slight problem. That transition from part-time to full-time? It involved doing something I'd never done before. It would also occupy more and more time doing something I wasn't good at and didn't enjoy. That Sunday night, as I drove home, I was impressed by the offer. By daylight Tuesday I was afraid of the job.

I don't mean nervous. I mean horrified.

Loathing.

Torn, in a way I had never experienced before.

You have to understand, I was the guy who had his destiny figured out. I was twenty years old and owned my future. At least I thought I did.

Until somebody offered me one that confused me.

In the wee hours of that Tuesday morning, for the only time I can remember, I dreamed in dread. Loathsome agony. All about this simple offer of a ministry position. And here was the rub: *I couldn't just say no.* I had the calling of God to deal with. Mentally I was in the Garden of Gethsemane with Jesus, and I'm quite sure about to sweat blood. I tossed and turned and languished and prayed, "Not my will, but thine, be done" (Luke 22:42, KJV).

After the sunrise gave me a reprieve, I hashed this whole thing out at the breakfast table with my mother. I know I'm making it sound like a big deal, but it took me five minutes to explain the dilemma. "They want me to do this, and I really don't want to do it. But my job isn't to do my will, but to do God's will."

Then she said the most profound thing I ever heard her say . . .

"Did it ever occur to you that God may be speaking to you through your desires?"

Cue the crickets. Stone-cold, baffled silence.

Well, *no*, actually, that never *had* occurred to me.

He can do that?

You mean, my will and God's will aren't always at war?

You mean, I have to completely rethink everything I understood about discipleship? And obedience? And callings and faith?

"I'll resign this weekend," I said.

Immediately I went from turmoil to peace.

That experience changed my future. More important, it changed my faith. I have since learned that, yes, God does often speak to you through your desires.

What do *you* want?

WHEN GOD INVADES YOUR PASSION

Having a son soon? Still pondering the little guy's name? Here's one for ya'—name him after that famous guy in the Bible. Call him Bezalel. Here's the press release from Moses:

> See, the LORD has called by name Bezalel the son of Uri, the son of
> Hur, of the tribe of Judah. And He has filled him with the Spirit of God,

in wisdom, in understanding and in knowledge and in all craftsman-
ship; to make designs for working in gold and in silver and in bronze,
and in the cutting of stones for settings and in the carving of wood, so
as to perform in every inventive work. He also has put in his heart to
teach, both he and Oholiab, the son of Ahisamach, of the tribe of Dan.
He has filled them with skill to perform every work of an engraver and
of a designer and of an embroiderer, in blue and in purple and in scarlet
material, and in fine linen, and of a weaver, as performers of every work
and makers of designs.

Exodus 35:30–35 (emphasis mine)

Did you see that? Here was a man who was anointed and pointed, wired and fired by the Holy Ghost!

For construction. Did you know that God can fill you with a supernatural love for things that get your hands dirty?

For art. Here was a man under the power of the presence of the Spirit, sent on a divine mission. The assignment—to carve wood and stone and form silver and gold and bronze.

For design. God gifted this man to do architectural and aesthetic things that had never been done before. And he was no specialist. He had the unction to function in every inventive work.

For needlework. Now hold on a minute. Aren't you gettin' a little girlie there, Lord? This guy invites his buddies over for a Spirit-led quilting party.

Then I love this phrase: God "has *put it in his heart* to teach." Bezalel felt the call to pass his anointed skills on to others.

Maybe you're still a little nervous when you apply this to your hard-core desires. How can I be sure that God is the one who put the passion there? How do I know it isn't my selfish desires? Let me give you the short answer for now:

He has made everything beautiful in its time. He has also set eternity
in the human heart.

Ecclesiastes 3:11, NIV

At the core of your being God has placed the *ultimate desire*. It's a longing for Him (see Psalm 84:2). Many addictions, compulsions, or unmet needs grow out of a spiritual yearning. Something's missing that can only be satisfied by Jesus Christ. We just try to fill it with the wrong stuff. That's why Jesus said,

> *"Anyone who is thirsty may come to me! Anyone who believes in me may come and drink! For the Scriptures declare, 'Rivers of living water will flow from his heart.'"*
>
> John 7:37–38, NLT

That tells me that He can be trusted with the desires of my heart. He understands them, despite how "unspiritual" they may appear. He also makes it clear that my ultimate fulfillment isn't in teaching, masonry, or even embroidery. They're in Him. If the passion doesn't flow into or out of intimacy with Jesus, it's worth a second look.

What if Bezalel lived today? What would God put in his heart to do? Maybe he'd be an anointed business consultant or troubleshooter. Perhaps a prophetic computer graphics designer or software engineer. How about a gifted school administrator, or a Spirit-filled firefighter? What if Bezalel was actually Bezalella? (Name your daughter that and I'll never admit in public that I know you!) What if her passion was to be a wife and mother? Or maybe she had an unction to function as an astronaut.

Bezalel does live today. If you know Jesus, you're him or her. You have a passion, and it's reflected in your desires and unique, God-given skills.

Sometimes, however, your passion sets you up for a fall. Desires are tricky. When our hearts are toward God, they point us in the direction we should be going. But when we fail to grasp the heart of our heavenly Father, those same desires can lead to bondage. We'll explore that more in the next section.

SEED MONEY

1. When you're feeling the most intimate with Jesus, what do you find yourself doing or wanting to do?

2. Do you find yourself looking at something in the future and you absolutely hate the idea? Do you find yourself torn between your will and God's? How can you sort out whether God can be speaking to you through your desires? What is the dreaded thing, and why do you dread it?

3. Read Colossians 1:9–12. How do you discover God's will for your life, and what is the result of walking in it?

4. What action step could you take in the next twenty-four hours that most resonates with your deepest desires toward God?

When Your Passion Is a Liar
Where Passion Meets Freedom

If only I could build an exit ramp. Something that would allow me to escape the rules and the never-ending expectations.

Why doesn't he realize I'm just not cut out for this kind of life? That he and I would both be happier if I were on my own?

Just once I'd like to remember what adrenaline feels like when it rushes through my veins.

Sound familiar? It should. Thoughts like these are repeated daily as people try to define freedom in their own terms.

We all long for authentic freedom. We want the power to make choices ourselves and live with joyful consequences. The good news of our relationship with Christ is that He came to set captives free! Unfortunately many believers fail to experience that freedom. Why? *Because they pursue a counterfeit form of freedom in one of two directions.*

In one of the most often-read stories in the Bible (Luke 15:11–32), Jesus reveals God's heart toward His children. It's the story of a father with two sons. The older one served his father faithfully for many years. The younger son was different; he longed to be free from his dad's authority.

Each son pursued and believed in his own passion. Neither understood the true heart of their father. While the father offered an abundant life of joy and liberty, each son pursued passion on his own terms. One sought it through pleasure, the other through performance. To the younger son, freedom meant *license* to do what he pleased. To the older brother, freedom meant *legalistic obedience* to the rules.

At any given time, you too can be a prodigal or a Pharisee. All it takes is a desire to find freedom apart from an intimate love relationship with God. That's when your passion becomes a liar.

FALSE FREEDOM IN A FAR COUNTRY

Two words sum up a prodigal's goal: personal gratification. A licentious person wants what he wants, when he wants it. His passion is for control over his own life. Many licentious people came from a strict background. Ever hear this phrase: "When I get out of this house . . ."?

Self-will at this level makes us slaves to impulsive and irresponsible decisions. Imagine the arrogance of a son who said, in effect, "Dad, I'd rather not wait until you die. I have plans, and I'd like to go ahead and take my inheritance now." For prodigals, the size and power of their passions leave them refusing to take "no" or "wait" for an answer.

I want it. Therefore I should have it.

Prodigals measure self-worth by satisfied desires. If they get what they want, right on time, then all is well and life is good. But sooner or later the party ends, the money runs out, and the friends evaporate. When that happens, sons begin thinking like hired servants. And in parable language, people become jealous of pigs. The prodigal becomes a loser in his own eyes.

This type of "freedom" only leads to more bondage. That's what all licentious prodigals have learned from Eden up to this moment. They eventually face the fact that they've been deceived. They ruthlessly pursue independence, with no restraint or authority. Yet in Paul's words, they "exchanged the truth of God for a lie" (Romans 1:25). Ultimately they don't break God's law; they break themselves on it—all the while pretending to be free.

THE OTHER BROTHER—THE OTHER DITCH

Far from the pigpen, another son pursued his own passion. He perceived himself to be living in loyal obedience to his father. But he knew no more of his father's love than his wandering sibling. No surprise, then, that he was offended at the party thrown for his rebellious brother. He was clueless about grace and jealous for his dad's approval. Some things never change.

Throughout history, many well-meaning people have missed the heart of the Father. All the while they've surrounded themselves with religious trappings. This describes the Pharisees Jesus often confronted, but it also could be describing you, even though nobody wants to admit they're a legalist.

Legalists look for a clear, uniform code to define how life should be lived. If they fail to find a clear code in the Bible, they invent some standard for *interpreting* the Bible.

Legalists keep their rules, follow the directions, and expect everyone else to do the same. Life is a checklist, and the solution to any problem is simple: work harder, do more good things, sin less.

Many legalists were once licentious. They've spent time in their own spiritual pigpen. But following their conversion or repentance, they sometimes go from one extreme to another.

Legalists are either hot or cold, all or nothing, with no middle ground. They measure their worth by their performance. They often carry a mental résumé of all the good things they've done. When pressed, they can repeat it back to God or whomever (see Luke 18:11–12). That's what makes this a more hideous form of bondage, because appearances are deceiving.

How can I be wrong when I'm acting so right?

How can I be in bondage when I compare so favorably to the pagans, or to my former life?

How can I be deceived when everyone around me tells me how well I'm doing?

The ultimate tragedy of the older brother is the price he paid to be correct. He sacrificed fellowship with the Father to maintain his life of calculated Christianity.

Judgmental and unforgiving, his life was littered with broken relationships. He was passionately religious, but miserable.

A NEW BIRTH OF FREEDOM

There in a pigpen, humbled but hopeful, a wandering son made a life-changing decision. "I'll get up and return to my father," he said (Luke 15:18, VOICE). Until then these brothers had one thing in common: *neither of them understood the heart of their Father.* You and I are often in the same trap.

Jesus reveals the Father as a face in the window—watching, waiting for His son to return.

He's an *embracer of the wanderer,* who runs to meet us when we make the first move toward Him.

He is a *redeemer of our lost identity,* who clothes us with the robe of sonship, despite how we may have abused it in the past.

He's a *party planner,* who throws raucous celebrations for wayward sons.

He's the *chief musician,* who dances with us and rejoices over us with singing (see Zephaniah 3:17).

He is a *boundless giver,* who said to His jealous son, "All I have is yours."

True freedom was there all along. Neither son experienced it—nor will we—until one was willing to leave his self-deception to find it. *The greatest investment you can make in your happiness and freedom is to trust that kind of God.*

The pardoned son had some lessons to learn. His brother did too, but never quite got it.

He learned that sons don't have to live like slaves, no matter what they've done in the past. The kingdom has no cheap seats, no second-class citizens.

He learned that you can't earn forgiveness. Otherwise it wouldn't be forgiveness! That wasn't good enough for the law-abiding brother. As a result, he never knew the truth, and it never set him free.

The pardoned son learned that your worth is measured by a Father who never stops loving you and watching for your return. One who will kiss you on your homecoming day and sacrifice His choice possession to throw you a party.

So how do you find freedom without being trapped by religion?

By humbling yourself and confronting the self-willed rebel you've become.

By receiving again the identity you own as God's child.

By rediscovering the role of celebration worship in revealing the heart of God.

By learning to live as a forgiven person.

And by realizing that all your longings are, indeed, longings for Him.

SEED MONEY

1. Read Luke 15;11–32. Pay attention to the actions and reactions of the father in the story. What do they tell you about the Lord's heart toward you?

2. Which character—the prodigal son, the older brother, or the pardoned son—do you relate to the most? Who in your life represents the other characters in the story and why?

3. How have you misunderstood God in the past? What images of God do you struggle with believing today?

4. What can you do to connect your desire for freedom to the Father's passionate love for you?

Do You See What He Sees?
Where Passion Meets Freedom

Ever read about the double-pump miracle Jesus performed? Fascinating story, about a blind man in Bethsaida. Jesus led him outside the village and spit on his eyes.

"Do you see anything?" He asked.

He looked up and said, "I see people; they look like trees walking around."

So Jesus double-clutched. Once more He put His hands on the man's eyes. This time the man saw everything clearly (see Mark 8:22–26, NIV).

It doesn't bother me that it took two rounds with the Son of God for a blind man to see clearly again. It *does* bother me that many of us have gone many rounds with Jesus, and we *still* don't see clearly at times.

He saw people that looked like trees. We see people that look like other things. We see jobs, economic status, social labels, racial stereotypes, gender. Jesus saw something else entirely. You can too, but it doesn't come naturally.

"I see people; they look like trees." What do you see? Butcher, baker, candlestick maker? Hot babe, geek, hero, freak? They may as well be Klingons, unless we learn to see from Jesus' perspective. We talk a lot about pursuing our own passions. But we can never fulfill our deepest passions unless we first embrace His. Where does *He* see the potential for abundance, influence, increase, and freedom? Take a look:

> *Jesus went around all the towns and villages, teaching in their synagogues, announcing the good news of the kingdom, and healing every disease and every sickness. When he saw the crowds, he felt deeply sorry for them, because they were distressed and dejected, like sheep without a shepherd. Then he said to his disciples, "There's plenty of harvest to be had, but not many workers! So pray the master of the harvest to send more workers to harvest his fields!"*
>
> Matthew 9:35–38, NTE

It doesn't take a PhD to recognize that Jesus saw something that moved Him, while the disciples missed it. What did Jesus see that seemed at once to tear His heart and excite His passion?

THE POVERTY

Jesus saw something different when He looked at people. "Harassed and helpless," describes one translation. "Weary and scattered," says another. A third calls them "distressed and dispirited." In short, Jesus saw the complete and utter spiritual poverty of humanity. He saw that the best efforts we could make to improve our situation are futile. Whatever you call happiness or success, if it cuts you off from a relationship with God, it's poverty!

Spiritual poverty comes in two forms: those who are desperately needy and know it and those who are desperately needy and *don't*. Those who acknowledge their need discover the kingdom of heaven (see Matthew 5:3).

But many people are blind to it—some by choice, others by ignorance. They may carry an air of respectability and goodness. But as we noted earlier, when God says you're busted, you're busted. It would be tragic enough if someone knew their desperate situation and saw no way out. It's beyond tragic if the solution is a prayer away, and they don't (or won't) see it.

Who are these people? Your neighbor. Your brother-in-law. Your bank teller. Your customer, employee, landlord, or tenant. Your boss. Your baby. Many of them are likable, even lovable. Many of them are also in spiritual poverty that calls you to action.

THE PERIL

"Sheep without a shepherd." That's quite a desperate situation when you realize sheep are the most helpless animals in the world. We were created to need a relationship with God. When we're living without one, it's not a pretty sight.

Sheep without shepherds can do some strange things. They think they can find their own way. They become driven by their bellies—always looking for a greener pasture. They become blind to danger, separated from other sheep.

Ever run into people who act like shepherdless sheep? You'll hear them say things like, "I can worship God anywhere—I don't need a church." Or "I have my own ideas about God." How about this classic: "It can't be wrong if it feels so right"?

I want to remind you what this looks like to the Son of God. Sheep without shepherds tear His heart out! I live in a Bible Belt American city of more than 200,000 people. Most of them don't have a personal relationship with Jesus. Add to that the many believers who wander around—independent, self-confident, or bitter. I'm telling you, it's breaking His heart!

What about your town? Your nation? Your neighborhood? You don't have the luxury of assuming they'll find their own way somehow. Left to their own direction, they face incredible danger.

Not later—now.

Not sometime—today.

THE POSSIBILITIES

Isn't it interesting that when Jesus saw those desperately needy people, He referred to them as a "harvest"? They may look like weeds to somebody else, but to Jesus they were the reason He came in the first place. Throughout His ministry Jesus saw ordinary people as harvest material. Peter and Andrew were fishermen. Jesus saw them as fishers of men. Matthew was a tax collector. Jesus saw him as a distributor of a new kind of wealth. John was a "Son of Thunder." Jesus saw him as the apostle of love. Now Jesus was looking at this crowd and saying, "There's a harvest." I don't think they saw it.

"Harvest? What harvest? That's Fred, the carpenter. That's Joe, the milkman."

"Harvest! Don't you mean, heathen? That's the local tax collector."

Two thousand years have come and gone, and it's still harvest time. The harvest is ready, whether you're ready or not. The harvest is ready, whether you're under stress or not. The harvest is ready, whether you feel adequate or not. There is always a way you can be involved. Don't you think that if it moved the heart of the Son of God that much, maybe it's that important?

THE PRIORITY

To Jesus the priority was and is always about people. Human nature is different. We value systems, forms, and things. Jesus values people. We see problems; Jesus sees people. We see labels; Jesus sees people. We see confusion and a need to control it; Jesus sees people, and a need to love.

So how do we focus on people? By doing the same thing Jesus did. Start with involvement. Jesus saw what He saw by doing something as simple as hanging out.

To your involvement, add understanding. Jesus took the time to understand people's hearts, not just their external appearances.

To your understanding, add intercession. Jesus prayed, and calls us to pray. And what we're praying for is *people*. The reason you may be praying for some things without an answer is that you're actually praying for *things*. You've made provision or guidance or your version of growth a *thing*. To God it's all about people.

So why *did* Jesus double-dip on that healing experience? To show us something about us. We get a touch from God and think we have the whole load. But we see people as objects, labels, or categories. What we need is another touch.

Maybe a touch of supernatural discernment. Or a touch of love and compassion. Or a touch of revelation. Or a touch of healing.

So how do you know if you need that second touch? Simple. If you really saw what He saw, you'd do what He did. You'd get involved in their lives. Care. Pray. Extend His healing.

One more thing. Regardless of your outward appearance, Jesus sees *your* heart. And that's a good thing! What He sees, He genuinely cares about. He sees your hurt. He sees your fear. He sees your stupid attempts to be your own shepherd. And it matters to Him. Would you let Him love you? Heal you? Save you? Forgive you? You're a harvest too, and the time is now.

SEED MONEY

1. Read Matthew 9:35–10:8. How did Jesus' perspective on the "harvest" affect His decision to send out the disciples? What ideas or principles do you see in His instructions to the disciples?

2. How do you tend to objectify people? Do you see them as race objects, religious objects, sex objects? How do you profile or prejudge people based on outward appearance?

3. How has involvement with different people or praying for them helped you understand them better?

4. Who can you engage with this week that you have tended to "see as trees walking"? How can you have a conversation with them or with God about them where your main task is to listen?

FINAL THOUGHT

Back to my dad and his pursuit of relationships. Even on his deathbed he found a way. We learned that despite his outward appearances of improvement, his lungs were continuing to deteriorate rapidly. But for two or three days he brightened up as he got to see all five of his grandchildren.

And he teared up when one of them told him that come November or December his eleventh great-grandchild would enter the world.

Know what he didn't talk about? His job. His career. His politics. But when he was staring at a face-to-face meeting with God, he did what he always did . . . He walked in the door. He made the call.

If my father's life still speaks today (and it does), it just isn't that complicated.

Walk in the door.

Make the call.

Follow your passion. It's a vital step in the LifeVesting cycle.

Hopefully by now you have a clearer view of your deepest values and desires. If not take some time to pray and process what God has placed in your heart. But don't settle for unfulfilled desires! In the next chapter we'll explore what it means to start realizing your own harvest. But you can't harvest if you don't plant. You can't plant if you don't have any seeds. So the next step is to allocate your resources.

CHAPTER 4

Allocate Your Resources

It's one thing to waste time or save time or for time to stand still.

I'm making up for *lost* time.

Literally.

I seem to have misplaced about four hours a couple of years ago and I *still* haven't gotten it back. Oh, I lived it. I was pretty agitated about it. I just can't remember it.

TIA, they called it. Which led to an MRI, an EEG, and a hospital with a big FEE. (I crack myself up.)

I was preparing to go deliver a final exam for a university class. Dressed and ready to go, tests in my hand, I went blank. Everything I know about the next four hours is what my wife told me. But apparently all I knew was, "I'm supposed to be somewhere, but I can't remember where."

That wasn't how I had planned my day. But life—and LifeVesting—has a way of throwing curves. And those curveball experiences are their own version of sowing and reaping.

NOT ALL REAPING IS WEEPING

Sometimes we assume that when we "reap what we sow" it's always bad news. Not so.

In a medical emergency, I was blessed to have somebody to call. Four times! I lit up my wife's phone while she was in a counseling session. (She was the counselor.) I don't remember any of that. What I vaguely *do* remember was calling her again when she was halfway home and her saying, "Just stay on the phone. I'm turning into the neighborhood."

A trip to the urgent care, where I flunked all the tests, led to the ER nearby. I don't remember much about any of that. But I'm told that when I saw my brother-in-law, I said, "I know you're my brother-in-law, but you're a lot uglier than I remember."

I guess some things get clearer in an emergency.

Anyway, in the hours that followed as I regained my wits (and wit), I had lots of visits. Our friend and pastor's wife stayed with us throughout. Another church pastor came. He and I did Michael Jackson and Bob Dylan imitations together in the ER (great fun). My stormtrooper daughter, who came in ready to take charge of the situation. My ever-present and not-as-ugly brother-in-law. My sister, nephew, and his wife. And a nonstop array of great medical professionals. Also several phone calls from and to the out-of-town kids to tell them to back away from the airport . . . don't come just yet.

All of that was the result of sowing somewhere along the line. I had taken time to sow into relationships. I had allocated money to sow into health insurance. I had taken energy and time to sow into the ministry of a local church. I had taken some emotional capital to sow into finding the funny in stressful times. So when the need came to withdraw on some of those deposits, the reaping was easy.

There was some hard reaping as well. Lots of silly talk about stress and lifestyle management. And, of course, the ever-present diet and exercise.

Frightening as it was, the experience demonstrated the power of sowing and reaping. Sowing intentionally into relationships. Sowing carelessly into high-risk health. It also called for a different kind of investing if I wanted to change my future. I was reminded again of the need to allocate my resources. To take part of my time, energy, relationships, and strength and invest it in a different result.

It doesn't take a medical crisis to learn to make disciplined, wise choices. In this chapter we'll dig deeper into the idea of setting part of your resources aside to invest in your future. Focusing on your calling or deepest passion will help you produce the results you yearn for. Discerning real value and avoiding stupid choices can change your life's direction. That's especially true when you learn to connect to God as your power source.

But allocating your resources starts by recognizing that your life is a trust, given to you by God Himself.

The Trust
Where Allocation Meets Abundance

"It all belongs to Jesus." We often use that phrase to refer to material things, but that's just a fraction of the scope of His possessions. Jesus owns all authority, wisdom, ability, honor, and praise. He owns all time and the material fullness of the earth. In fact, every currency we need to survive and thrive is a commodity that rightfully belongs to Him. If you need it, He owns it.

You and I belong to Him too. But in a strange twist of providence, He allows us to choose our highest values, even if He's at the bottom of our list.

> *"You see, the kingdom of heaven is like a man going on a journey.*
> *He called his servants and entrusted his possessions to them."*
> Matthew 25:14, EHV

That's how Jesus describes your life in light of the kingdom of heaven. It's a *trust*—a relationship in which God is the owner and you make the management decisions. In the story of the talents, each of the servants received part of the master's possessions to manage for him. That represents your life and all it entails. None of that is yours. Jesus purchased it (see 1 Corinthians 6:19–20) and entrusted it to you to manage.

This parable of the talents is about the sum of all the factors that make up your life. Each servant in the story received a unique "portfolio," and so did you. Your life is a unique blend of characteristics. That includes your natural abilities, spiritual gifts, relationships, intelligence, material possessions, and more. No one in the world has the unique blend you do. You don't even have the same portfolio you had a year ago! That's why it's vain to compare yourself with somebody else.

Your life is also an *opportunity*—an avenue through which God wants to bless you. As in the parable, God gave you the life you have to bless you. That doesn't come only from the trust itself but also from what you do with what He gives you. Unfortunately not everyone sees it that way. Some people become life hoarders (as in the story here), consumers, gamblers, or pleasers.

So what determines your portfolio? Why do you have what you have? Why is it different than it was a year ago? Why is it different from other people? The short answer, of course, is God. The "stuff" is His, and He can do anything He wants with it. But certain clues in the story help us better understand our LifeVesting opportunities.

YOUR ABILITY

"Dividing it in proportion to their abilities," Jesus said (Matthew 25:15, TLB). Your abilities involve your spiritual gifts, natural abilities, acquired skills, and education. Many abilities are subject to the law of use ("use it or lose it"). I discovered that a few years ago when I tried to play softball for the first time in nineteen years. It was ugly.

Here's a phrase I hear often: "God won't give me more than I can handle." Interesting, though, that usually the person who says that is dealing with some form of unending stress. I've never heard a lottery winner say that. I've never heard the breathless couple shout that phrase from the limo as they leave the wedding. Why is it that we only talk about God and what we can handle in the context of tough stuff?

Come on, admit it. How many times have you sputtered to the Lord *all the good things* you could do if you had that million or two in the bank? Or that position of power or authority? Yet heaven is silent. Think about this for a while: maybe you *can't* handle it—*if so, you'd have it*. That doesn't mean you can *never* handle it. Only that the trust God has given you reflects your ability. If you want a greater trust, as much as is in your power, get greater ability. And remember, as you grow and mature, sometimes the only thing missing is time.

OUR PREVIOUS USE OF RESOURCES

> *"His master praised him for good work. 'You have been faithful in
> handling this small amount,' he told him, 'so now I will give you many
> more responsibilities. Begin the joyous tasks I have assigned to you.'"*
>
> Matthew 25:21, TLB

These words are both haunting and exciting. They're haunting because of the many little "small amounts" I've mishandled along the way. They're exciting because of the opportunities we have daily to rise to the opportunities at hand. You may not be able to change your past but you *can* redefine it. Will Rogers once said, "Good judgment comes from experience, and a lot of that comes from bad judgment." Yesterday's mistakes can be today's lessons; they don't have to be today's habits.

LifeVestors help create their future by how they manage today's realities. Have you ever decided you were too important, too smart, too big for the small assignment that fell in your lap? Have you ever said to yourself that when you get that big opportunity, you'll *really* shine? You may want to rethink that. In God's economy, the way to get where you're going is to be faithful where you are, even in the days of small things.

THE UNCERTAINTY OF THE SEASON

Your portfolio is determined by how you manage uncertainty. Jesus had a lot of things to say about that. The uncertainty of your life makes the trust God has given you both urgent and important. Just like the parable, the greater trusts are given to those who show they can "redeem the time" (see Ephesians 5:16).

Your timeline comes with no guarantees. You have an appointment with God but no clue about the day and hour. And when God calls your name, that's it. It will be too late to pray, to turn your life around, to mend that broken relationship.

I've had too many classmates die and conducted the funerals of too many minors not to see the urgency of this. "Night is coming when no one can work," Jesus said (John 9:4). Your good intentions are cheap. The urgency of LifeVesting is in the fact that your days are uncertain—and limited.

YOUR CONFIDENCE IN GOD

In the parable, the LifeVestors put their "talents"—their unique relationship with the owner—to work. Jesus used the word *traded*. When you put money, time, or relationships to work, it's an exchange. You offer something of value in exchange for something of value, trusting that it will produce an increase. Farmers do that with seed. Investors do that with real estate or equity in a company. People do that with their education and relationships too.

But what made the LifeVestors different from the hoarder? You'll find the answer in the hoarder's mousy excuse:

> *"Sir, I knew you were a hard man, and I was afraid you would rob me of what I earned."*
>
> Matthew 25:24, TLB

He didn't trust him, so the hoarder didn't act with his master's authority, seek his master's glory, or trust his master's intentions. He "played it safe"—and insulted his leader.

When you trust God enough to use His authority as His ambassador, every-thing changes. When you put the trust He has given you to work, you're express-ing one of the highest forms of worship. You are saying with your life, "I trust You enough to seek Your pleasure." And God trusts someone who trusts Him like that.

In the next section I'll show you a shortcut to identifying what your trust actually is. You may be surprised.

SEED MONEY

1. Read Matthew 25:14–30. If your life was one of the three managers in the story, what's in your portfolio? What has your "master" (God) entrusted to you? Talents? Finances? Possessions? Relationships? What would prompt Him to say "Well done!" to you for how you managed your portfolio?

2. "The adventure of LifeVesting is in the urgency of the fact that your days are uncertain—and limited." What have you put off that you would regret leaving undone if your time on earth was up?

3. What are the "little things" you're handling that you hope to be "bigger things"? How can you continue to be faithful without "borrowing from the future"?

4. Write out a prayer in which you specifically commit to the Lord to be faithful with today's assignment(s) for you.

Have You Written Your Opus?
Where Allocation Meets Leadership

"Something's wrong with your work," the superior said.

The subject in the job review was a faithful old pastor. The superior was a member of the denomination's hierarchy.

"Only one convert has been added to your church this year, and he is only a boy," the boss said.

Later that same day the pastor was alone in his study, praying with a heavy heart, when someone walked up behind him. Turning around, he saw the boy—his only convert that year. "Pastor, do you think I could become a preacher or a missionary?" he asked.

That boy was Robert Moffatt, who became the missionary who later opened Africa to the gospel. Years later he was speaking in London where a young doctor was in the audience. "I have seen in the morning sun the smoke of a thousand villages where no missionary has ever been," Moffatt said. The doctor, deeply moved by Moffatt's message, was David Livingstone. In 1840 Livingstone sailed for Africa, where he labored for more than thirty years.

Back to that pastor. Was he a success? Was he significant? I guess it all depends on whether you're adding or multiplying. On a surface level he didn't have much by way of statistics to advertise. Fortunately God keeps a different scorebook.

Never has the world seen a generation more intoxicated with success. Nothing wrong with the desire, in and of itself. I don't know of anybody who draws near to the throne every morning by praying, "Lord, please make me a failure today." The problem comes when Christians use faulty standards to measure their success. When we do that, we sow the seeds of our own discouragement and worthlessness.

Ultimately your success will be measured by two things: how you allocated your time and how you responded to your calling.

THE CLOCK IS TICKING

I had a moving experience a few years ago on a lazy Sunday afternoon. I'd seen the movie *Mr. Holland's Opus* several years earlier, and for whatever reason decided to watch it again. At the end, Mr. Holland, who had been a band director and music teacher, sees the lives he's changed. And he hears the governor, once his student, say, "Mr. Holland, we are your opus."

My gut turned inside out. It hit a nerve—a deep, raw nerve—like nothing had in years, perhaps ever. There in the den I sat, alone in the house, sobbing. Crying out to God. *"Oh God, I want to have that kind of impact on other people's lives."*

What surprised me wasn't the desire; that's been a staple of my life for years. It was the *force* of it. I want to get to the end of my life and see that I have made that kind of difference. I want it badly. Deeply. And somewhere in my heart of hearts, at least on that day, I didn't feel as though I had.

In the movie, Glen Holland put his own dreams aside year after year to invest in his students and family. All the time he originally budgeted for composing—his own personal dream—was sucked up in making a living. But his living was teaching. He gave his students knowledge and, more important, a moral compass for using it. All those years, he saw himself as a guy who endured the sacrifices necessary to make a living. He had swallowed the disappointment of a life of unfulfilled dreams. What he didn't realize was that in giving up his *ambition*, he'd found a *calling*. He never realized how much it meant to him until someone took it away. He also never realized how much he'd meant to his students.

The movie quoted a famous line from John Lennon: "Life is what happens while you're making other plans." It's there that callings are often found and other lives are affected. Many Christians waste their time pining away for the magic moment that is neither magic nor a moment. Meanwhile life grinds on. But here's where we miss it: *God is in the grind!* James puts it this way:

> *You do not even know what will happen tomorrow. What is your life? You are a mist that appears for a little while and then vanishes.*
>
> James 4:14, NIV

I want to do something with my "mist." I want to use the time I have to impact a new generation. I'll quit pining away for something I may never see. I'll view today's sacrifices and necessities as the means through which I make my greatest impact. And I'll offer my time, gifts, and attention to those who otherwise seem to be inconveniences.

How about you?

WHERE IS YOUR FIELD?

You may not be the next darling of the press or the name-droppers club. You may not receive lots of shiny awards or public attention. Like Mr. Holland, you may find yourself disposable—a cultural throwaway. But none of that matters in the long run. Conventional wisdom and public opinion have never been the measure of real success. And they never will.

Behind the headlines and notice of the crowd, something extraordinary is taking place. Week in and week out, countless people make a difference for the long haul. They endure long days of service with little encouragement and no worldly attainment. And that's nothing new. Men and women who love Christ and love people have devotedly carried heavy burdens for generations. In churches and schools, homes and hospitals, they show up and stand a post. Let one of them take a tumble, and you'll hear about it everywhere. Otherwise their stories of sacrifice and service never make headlines.

However, they capture God's attention. He keeps score a different way. Many unsung heroes will leave this life feeling hardly noticed, much less effective. Yet their lack of recognition and rewards entitles them to another kind of renown. And this one comes from the Lord Jesus Himself.

When John Wesley died, he didn't leave much behind. Only two silver spoons, his glasses, preaching bands, cloak, prayer book, and the typical odds and ends. Fortunately he had also preserved his writing. Today his journals, letters, essays, sermons, and tracts live on for later generations. More than that, Wesley left the legacy of a faithful life lived in service to his God.

> *"Who is the dependable manager, full of common sense, that the master puts in charge of his staff to feed them well and on time? He is a blessed man if when the master shows up he's doing his job."*
>
> Luke 12:42–43, MSG

My responsibility and yours is to leave a heritage of faithfulness with our time and our calling. If you'll trust the results to God, then a ripe harvest of influence awaits you. Even if it seems obscure and unimportant to the world, in God's economy it's priceless. Write your opus! Leave a legacy! In doing so, your influence will shine bright for generations to come. And as you'll see in the next section, you'll point those generations to where the real value lies.

SEED MONEY

1. Read Luke 12:35–48. What does faithfulness have to do with accountability and preparation to meet the Lord? How do faithful servants behave?

2. "The problem comes when Christians use faulty standards to measure their success and sow the seeds of their own discouragement and worthlessness." How might you get down on yourself because you don't measure up to the world's success standards?

3. List some of the people you have the opportunity to influence in the "routine and insignificant" grind of your life?

4. What specific way can you reach out to that person or persons this week and serve them simply and practically?

How to Find Real Value
Where Allocation Meets Increase

Things got a little weird at the Taco Bell in Fond du Lac, Wisconsin. A customer tried to use two 1928 five-dollar bills as cash to pay for his meal. The clerks had never seen such old money before, presumed it to be counterfeit, and called the police. Here's the sad part—as currency the cash was legit. As collectors' items they were worth more than a burrito combo or chalupa.

What a waste, right? Right up there with Esau selling his birthright for a bowl of peas (see Genesis 25:31–34). Or the prodigal son wasting his inheritance on a never-ending party (see Luke 15:13).

But another part of my brain wants to defend our fast-food shopper. After all, maybe he was hungry, and that was the only cash he had. Maybe he had no idea what he had. I've learned that if you don't know the value of what you have, it doesn't matter to you what you waste it on. Esau and the prodigal learned that too—the hard way.

Life presents a daily cornucopia of possibilities, opportunities, and choices. They all demand our allegiance and ask to be a priority. With all that's possible—the bad, the good, the best—how do we keep from squandering the most valuable pieces of our lives? It's one thing to allocate our resources. It's another to invest in the ones with the most value. In a world of multiple-choice-gone-crazy, how do we choose well? By discerning the time and identifying God's high-value targets.

GOD SPEAKS THROUGH JUNK MAIL

It was a typical piece of junk mail—the next great offer, last of the big bargains, something like that. Right before it sailed off into file-13 history, something at the bottom of the page caught my eye. It read:

Four things that you can never get back . . . the spoken word . . . your past life . . . wasted time . . . and neglected opportunity.

Never has something so near oblivion been so profound. Some parts of our lives are like the tides. So much comes, goes, comes back again. But other parts are like a shooting star—they never come back. Other chances may come that look similar, but that's only a matter of appearance. Fact is, there are four things you can never get back—four times when your LifeVesting choices matter more.

You can never get back *the words you've spoken.* That's what makes them so powerful. That's what makes angry words so destructive, and untrue words so demoralizing. It's also what makes kind words such a healing force. Every time you inhale and part your lips to speak, you're writing your message on the hearts of the listener. And once written, your words can never be erased.

You can never get back *your past life.* That works on both ends. Your days of glory and your days of pain. Your triumphs and your trauma. Your victories and your failures. What's in the past can never be changed. You can't pretend the bad things didn't happen. You can't deny the good you've done either. Painfully, sometimes cruelly, life goes on and demands that you go on with it. You can learn and grow from your past or be condemned to repeat it. But you can't get it back.

You can never get back *the time you have wasted.* That's why the Bible talks about "redeeming the time." Have you ever wondered why the days seem to go by faster as we get older? Maybe it's because age teaches us to recognize how short life is and how much time we have wasted. Pablo Picasso said it a long time ago: "Only put off for tomorrow what you are willing to die having left undone."

You can never get back *your neglected opportunities.* Others may come back in a familiar form, but doors of opportunity are only open for a season. And those doors will eventually close—either behind you or before you. The only difference is where you are standing when it closes. The roads to hell, heartache, and hopelessness have been paved with the sad words "If only."

DISCERNING THE PRICELESS FROM THE PLASTIC

"Isn't there more to life than this?" A common question about a host of things. It's also a rhetorical question Jesus Himself asked. He was speaking to a group of people who worried and fretted about their "stuff" (see Matthew 6:19–34). In His love and wisdom, Jesus gave some hints about how we can find real value in our decisions and priorities.

Central to all He said is this core principle: *you can change your destiny and your results by changing your values.* If you aren't satisfied with where you are or where you're going, you're going to have to change what's most important to you. According to Jesus, real value revolves around five principles.

Security

> *"Store your treasures in heaven, where they will never become moth-eaten or rusty and where they will be safe from thieves."*
>
> Matthew 6:20, NLT

Real value is found in things that neither time nor thieves can take away. To determine the value of a possession, a commitment, a relationship, look at it in light of the long run.

Service

Why did Jesus say you can't serve two masters—particularly God and money (see Matthew 6:24)? Because real value is found in what you're serving and what's serving you. Because I value my children, I serve them. What's more, we let them serve us in ways we don't necessarily allow others to do. It's an expression of value. You serve what matters to you. If you want different results, change who or what you're serving.

Self

> *"There is far more to your life than the food you put in your stomach, more to your outer appearance than the clothes you hang on your body. . . . And you count far more to him than birds."*
>
> Matthew 6:25–26, MSG

Real value starts with realizing your worth to God. That's the only way you can be free from worry and anxiety. It's also the only way you'll have the courage to make changes in your life.

Source

> *"What I'm trying to do here is to get you to relax, to not be so preoccupied with getting, so you can respond to God's giving."*
> Matthew 6:31, MSG

The source of the benefit determines its value. That's why I value a gift from my wife more than one from a stranger. So is it possible to position yourself in such a way that you are receiving directly from God? Yes. More on that later.

Society

"The Gentiles eagerly seek all these things," Jesus said (Matthew 6:32). In other words, this stuff is cheap. Common. Everybody's chasing it. Real value is found in rarity—in this case, how distinct you are from the world. This principle rings true in the stock market, the antique store, and your mother's advice. If everybody's buying it, perhaps you should question it.

Not everything that's pricey from a material standpoint is valuable. Solomon's haunting reflection still rings true today:

> *Everything I wanted I took—I never said no to myself. I gave in to every impulse, held back nothing. I sucked the marrow of pleasure out of every task—my reward to myself for a hard day's work!*
> *Then I took a good look at everything I'd done, looked at all the sweat and hard work. But when I looked, I saw nothing but smoke. Smoke and spitting into the wind. There was nothing to any of it. Nothing.*
> Ecclesiastes 2:10–11, MSG

So how can *you* find real value? Think through these five value questions when you're presented with the next great "can't miss" opportunity.

- Will it last? Does it have staying power?
- Who or what do I want to serve, or have serving me?
- If I believed with confidence that God sees me as priceless, what would I pursue with my life?
- How can I position myself to receive from God as my primary source?
- How exceptional is this?

Learn to recognize your shooting stars. Learn to discern what's really valuable. And when you find it, have enough resources available to seize it. There are no guarantees it will be there tomorrow. But as will see, some "opportunities" are dangerous snares in disguise.

SEED MONEY

1. Read Matthew 6:19-34. What did Jesus tell us not to do or not to worry about? What did He say to focus on? What does this tell you about finding real value?

2. In the spirit of that famous commercial line "What's in your wallet?"— what are your most cherished and valuable possessions, tangible and intangible? Why are they so valuable to you?

3. The roads to hell, heartache, and hopelessness have been paved with the sad words "If only." If you could undo one bad choice or wasted opportunity from the past and redo it, what would you bring back? What would you do differently?

4. What one action step can you take to shift your focus away from the worrisome and trivial to where real value lies?

The Fury of the Moment
Where Allocation Meets Freedom

Take an imaginary trip with me to a pacing place. Back and forth. Back and forth. Pacing.

He was restless. Bored with the battlefield, if you could imagine that. He was everybody's darling—the "Shepherd of Israel," they called him. Living proof that good guys really can come in first, even if they weren't born into it.

His thoughts weren't racing—they were pacing. "I know I ought to go to work, but I'm just not motivated. Anyway, the army's in good hands. They don't need me. I think I'm entitled to some time for myself."

This was a time when the Shepherd of Israel should have been shepherding. No one could fulfill his responsibility but him. This was a time—a pacing time— when danger didn't look dangerous. But what's that thing your Grandma used to say about idle minds and the devil's workshop? Yeah, that.

Up from his afternoon nap one lazy day, he takes a stroll along the roof of the palace. Pacing. From his vantage point, he sees a woman bathing. She's stunning. Drop-dead gorgeous. But he's seen women before, and if he may say so himself, he knows how to treat a woman. Unlike some of the lugs and thugs he's come across in his day. So to a pacing heart, seeing this one is no big deal.

This is when the giant slayer should flee, because this is a different kind of giant. The first look may be unavoidable. The second is irresistible. Being in authority doesn't make him immune from disaster. Nor does it entitle him to violate the trust of those who served him. But pacing hearts miscalculate their situation and their strength.

Still, he loves God. After all, he's the chief musician, the worship innovator. When he prays, God talks back. He has mastered his spirit and ruled over his desire for revenge. Yet he has also broken forth in amazing free and spontaneous public worship. He's a giant killer with a giant heart for God.

So where's God now?

"Oh," he says, "God understands. I'll deal with Him later."

If ever he needs to deal with God, it's *now*. Not after he's made a tragic mistake. He should talk to God *before* he screws up. There's more to grace than covering failure. The Lord also offers strength to avoid stupid choices in the first place.

But the pacing king rationalizes that God isn't the issue. He forgets that *if you're in covenant with God, then God is always the issue.*

"Make the call. Find out who she is. No, no, I'm just curious. But while you're at it, ask her to join me in the palace for, uh, dinner. That's it. Dinner."

Still his heart paces. He should turn back. There's still time. Cancel the stupid call. Cancel dinner. He could fast and pray instead. He could send an embarrassed and humble apology for the misunderstanding. Hey, he could invite his own wife to dinner, not somebody else's. He could court her. Tell her how grateful he is for her.

Fast forward—too late now. We have a "situation."

Let's see if he can fix this. Her husband will be an honorable victim. She'll be the grieving widow. He'll be the comforting friend, and they'll be proud parents. Hey, all's well that ends well. No point hurting more people than needed. After all, he feels bad about this but can't undo what's been done.

Anyway, he has to think of what's good for the country.

However sad the situation, he'll have plausible deniability. "I'm not there, so it's not my fault." Blinded by that excuse, he kills his friend with the sword of his enemy.

His pacing heart knows better. He knows better because he's walked with God long enough. This calls for confession, not more image management. Manipulation is participation, even when you're nowhere near the crime scene. Any way he slices it, covering up his sin won't prosper him (see Proverbs 28:13). Committing more sin to cover up previous sin *certainly* won't prosper him. If he were concerned about the good of the country, he wouldn't have toyed with the temptation in the first place. He isn't protecting anything but his own charming reputation.

Fast-forward. He had believed the lies. Sucker punched by his own indulgence. He believed that covered sin is forgotten sin. He had convinced himself that all was well because no one had confronted him with it. He believed wrong. They didn't have personal injury attorneys around back then, but they did have prophets. And the voice still rings in his ears: "Thou art the man" (2 Samuel 12:7, KSV).

There's nothing covered up that won't be revealed. Jesus said that (see Luke 12:2). David lived it and so will you and I. We have no control over how that gets revealed—only how we respond when it is. We could rationalize with our rational lies. Or we could embrace the life-giving power of truth, however hard it may be in the short run.

David chose truth. "Okay, I was wrong," he says. "I have sinned."

And he is forgiven. But there's hell to pay, starting with the death of the "situation." He will have war and rebellion in his own household as long as he lives. For a year, David had believed the stupid, stupid idea that his failure didn't affect anybody but him. Wrong again. Some blunders reap a whirlwind that devastates an entire family or a whole nation. Even sometimes generations to come.

Yes, sin has consequences. But grace has even greater, more wonderful consequences. Yet David will be challenged for the rest of his life to receive grace and live like a forgiven man.

But here's the wonder of grace. Soon another baby would arrive. Same dad. Same mother. But in a move only grace can explain, this son was handpicked by God to be Israel's next king. And through this same fallen shepherd who received God's grace, generations later, the Son of God entered the world. Jesus, Son of David. Regardless of the impact of sin, the impact of grace will always be greater (see Romans 5:20).

Fast-forward again. He's heaving and shaking uncontrollably now. Doubled over with unspeakable pain. The death of an infant had rocked his world. But this? The death of a son he never could reach, no matter how hard he tried? It has shattered his life. And he paces again, the crushed, mournful walk of regret and sorrow.

"O my son! My son Absalom! Absalom, my son!
If only I had died in your place, my son! Absalom, my son!"

You think he ever stopped to gaze at a woman bathing again? You think he ever blew off his responsibility to his mighty men, his warriors, ever again? To his credit, no. He never repeated the same mistake twice. That's one reason God referred to him as a man after His own heart.

Fast-forward one more time. That special son, the grace-king, now sits on the throne. One night, in the quiet, he rests after dedicating the temple his father envisioned. He rests but he can't sleep. Pacing.

He has a divine visitor.

"As for you, if you walk before me faithfully as David your father did . . . I will establish your royal throne, as I covenanted with David your father when I said, 'You shall never fail to have a successor to rule over Israel.'"

2 Chronicles 7:17–18, NIV

Wait, what? Walk before me faithfully as *who*? David? That liar? That adulterer? That murderer? What did He mean by that?

At any given point in this story, David could have allocated different resources. In doing so he would have created different outcomes. The measure of a man or woman is not what we do in the fury of the moment. What matters is what we do in the grace of a lifetime.

We weren't made to live without the power of God. Sometimes we need it to guard against temptations. At other times we need it to press toward a desired future. As you'll see in the next section, God's power isn't something we get "out there" or "up there." It's at work in you this very moment.

SEED MONEY

1. Read Psalm 51. What had David learned from his failure, and how did he respond to it?

2. Some people have a problem with leaders and believers who fail greatly. Others have an even greater problem with a God who forgives even more greatly. How do you feel about God's grace? Do you have a hard time accepting it, either for yourself or for someone else? Why?

3. He "believed the stupid, stupid idea that his failure didn't affect anybody but him." How have your failures affected others? How have the failures of others affected you?

4. What will you do to live out the grace of God or walk in forgiveness this week?

Connecting to God as Your Power Source
Where Allocation Meets Eternity

Locked out again. For the third time! From my own house! It wasn't that I didn't have keys; I did. Key to the back deadbolt—check. Key to the front door—check. But if Robin had locked the exterior front door and the doorknob (a different key) in the back as she left, I was done for.

This time it got interesting. I had to explain to the local policeman why I was picking the lock at this house. Turns out he actually helped me pick the lock and get inside. But still, I was embarrassed at having to explain myself to law enforcement.

Eventually we moved. My last act in leaving town was to drop my keys off at the now-empty house and head out. Walking through one last time, I looked at the keys I'd left on the kitchen counter. I noticed a key I had never used before and got curious. What lock did that key open?

You know where this is going, don't you?

Sure enough, it was the key to the back doorknob. And I'd carried it in my pocket the whole time!

Talk about living below my privilege. But that's nothing compared to the experience of many believers, including me. We have our own versions of being "locked out," assuming we have no way to solve the problem. All the while we're holding the key we need.

The greatest resource you can allocate in pursuing a God-sized vision is the power of God Himself. Yet many believers have been locked out of their own lives of blessing because they pursued dreams and goals in their own way. If Jesus came to give you an abundant life, doesn't it make sense to seek Him for that life of abundance?

As I learned the hard way, having the key doesn't guarantee unlocking the door. I had to *appropriate* what the key could do for me. The same is true in pursuing your vision. Having God's resources as your birthright still requires you to learn to exercise them.

THERE *IS* A POWER AT WORK IN YOU

The apostle Paul used vivid language to describe how he prayed for the believers in Ephesus:

> *For this reason I bow my knees before the Father, from whom every*
> *family in heaven and on earth is named, that according to the riches*
> *of his glory he may grant you to be strengthened with power through*
> *his Spirit in your inner being, so that Christ may dwell in your hearts*
> *through faith—that you, being rooted and grounded in love, may have*
> *strength to comprehend with all the saints what is the breadth and length*
> *and height and depth, and to know the love of Christ that surpasses*
> *knowledge, that you may be filled with all the fullness of God.*
>
> *Now to him who is able to do far more abundantly than all that we*
> *ask or think, according to the power at work within us, to him be glory*
> *in the church and in Christ Jesus throughout all generations, forever and*
> *ever. Amen.*
>
> Ephesians 3:14–21, ESV

Regardless of your feelings or experience, God's limitless power works non-stop in you. This power exceeds anything we can imagine. Paul uses phrases like "the riches of his glory" to describe it. It's a reflection of an all-powerful Christ who can blow your mind by what He's capable of doing.

Want to know a secret? *This is an inside job.* It takes place in your "inner being." In you. Hopelessly human you! Which means that before God shows His power in your universe, He shows His power in you. Before He changes your circumstances, He changes you. *This is one of the reasons so many Christians remain powerless.* We want God to change the outward view but don't want Him to change us in the process.

PLUGGING INTO THE POWER

If this power is readily available like the electrical current in your house, how do we plug into it? Paul mentions three "outlets"—faith, love, and community—where we connect to this limitless power.

Start with faith. One of Jesus' most-repeated messages during His ministry was *Believe!* When Jesus said *all things* are possible when you believe (see Mark 9:23), He meant it. The greater your confidence in God's faithfulness, the greater your experience of God's power.

Look closely. Right now God has you in a place where He's calling you to trust Him. It may be your finances or your relationships. It could be your career or your health. Regardless, the question remains, will you trust Him? Will you take what He freely offers? Will you yield to His will? Will you rest on His promises? Jesus said something both hopeful and haunting—"According to your faith let it be done to you" (Matthew 9:29, NIV).

Love is the second connecting point. Through love we are "rooted and grounded." When we know by experience the love of Christ, it surpasses all other kinds of understanding. And love is our gateway to all the fullness of God.

The greatest displays of God's power in your life involve receiving and expressing His love. This is a love that bears a cross for sinners. That touches lepers and blesses rejects. This love forgives failed followers and heals broken lives. If you're living a powerless life, you're likely missing the love connection somewhere.

The third point of connection to God's power is community. "With all the saints" we come to know the love and fullness of Christ. Everything God makes available to us is in the context of community relationships. You may not like that idea, but it's still true. God's glory is revealed in connection with His church. In other words, there is no "self-vesting" without "we-vesting."

When believers walk in unity and focus first on others, we position ourselves to connect with God's power. Simply put, none of us was made to survive by flying solo. If you want to engage the fullness of God's power, you'll have to engage in the fellowship of God's people.

FLIPPING THE SWITCH

Faith, love, and community describe states of relationship that connect us to God's power. But what do we do to allocate it? Try following Paul's example— prayer and praise.

"For this reason, I bow my knees," Paul said. Paul *wanted* something from the Lord, so he earnestly asked for it. "You do not have because you do not ask"

(James 4:2). And that's what Paul did. He asked, ultimately, that the Ephesians would be filled with all of God's fullness. That's a high-protein prayer!

Paul's prayer was focused outward. He was praying for their faith, love, and community. That doesn't mean it's wrong to ask for personal needs. But here the needs of others were being raised to God by a man who was in prison. Paul wasn't asking for his release. He was praying for their revelation and power.

Praise also flips the switch. Paul breaks into celebration worship as he imagines God responding to His prayer. In fact, before they ever experienced the power, Paul praised God as if the power had already arrived. Your expressions of worship, gratitude, and celebration to God can do the same thing.

Praise is the highest expression of faith, love, and community. When you worship God devotedly, you declare your confidence in Him. You receive and share His love. And you join with the larger body of Christ all over the world in declaring the worth of your God.

There's power in that. There's power at work right now in you. But you must plug into it and flip the switch. Or put another way, you have the key. But to unlock the door to God's power, you must use it.

SEED MONEY

1. Read Ephesians 3:14–21 again and do a Trinity study. What does Paul say about the Father? What does he write about Christ the Son? What does he say about the Holy Spirit? And what does each have to do with you?

2. How have you experienced a need for God's power or a reminder of your own powerlessness lately?

3. What vision or dream do you have that can only be realized by God's power at work in you? How can you turn that dream into prayer for others and praise for who God is now?

4. "Look closely. Right now God has you in a place where He is calling you to trust Him." Where do you see the Lord calling out faith in you? How can you demonstrate faith in that area?

FINAL THOUGHT

Back to the hospital. While I was there, I had a nice long visit with my pastor and friend, Alan. We talked a lot about where to go from there. It was encouraging but hard.

It was encouraging because he reminded me that I still have a future and a hope. And he encouraged me to dream. This book is a partial fulfillment of that dream.

It was hard because in all the going and going, I didn't feel I had the mental or emotional muscles to dream anymore. I had to learn to develop and flex those muscles again. That, my friend, is why I call it a LifeVesting *cycle*. I had to learn to explore the possibilities again.

My son Joel asked me the most dreaded question of anybody in any form of ministry . . . *Do you have a day off?* It was encouraging but hard.

It was encouraging because he reminded me I am still part of God's strategy to redeem the world. It was hard because I have a bias toward action and want to be doing stuff every day. But when God said to work six days, not seven, He didn't pin a cape on me and give me a pass. In God's economy you can't allocate time for work without also allocating time to invest in rest.

So the first thing I did when I left the hospital—after repeatedly saying "thank you" to lots of people—is nothing.

N-O-T-H-I-N-G.

For six hours anyway. And strangely enough, it felt OK.

CHAPTER 5

Execute Your Plan

S uppose you could travel back in time and witness some event as it happened. What would you like to see firsthand?

My family and I played that "what if" game on a trip a few years ago. There were the obvious answers, of course. To see the Red Sea divided into two walls of water. To witness the resurrection or ascension of Jesus. To hear Lincoln's Gettysburg address.

Lately I've been working on another list, because it speaks not just to the past but also to my future and yours.

If I could be a fly on history's wall, here are some things I'd like to see, in no certain order:

- I'd love to see Walt Disney show his wife the sketch of a cartoon mouse he drew on the train ride home—one he called "Mortimer." Lillian had a better idea. "Call him Mickey," she said.
- I'd love to see Oprah Winfrey's first screen test.
- I'd love to hear Billy Graham the first time he ever stood to preach.
- I'd love to see Norman Vincent Peale's wife, Ruth, mail his book manuscript to yet another publisher. It was still in the trash can because he

forbade her to take it out. So she mailed it, trash can and all. (The book was *The Power of Positive Thinking*. It sold thirty million copies.)

- I'd love to see Rick Warren knock on that first California door and ask, "Do you go to church anywhere around here? Why not?"
- I'd love to see Fanny Crosby writing her first poem.
- I'd love to see Paul W. Bryant wrestle that bear and earn a nickname for life.
- I'd love to see the Wright Brothers flip the coin to see who would pilot that contraption first.
- I'd love to see John Hancock be the first to sign the Declaration of Independence.
- I'd love to see Martin Luther nailing his *Ninety-five Theses* to the Wittenberg Chapel door.
- I'd love to see Moses, with a still-hot rod in his hand, explain to his wife exactly why he had to return to Egypt.
- I'd love to see David's face turn red when he first heard about that taunting giant and decided that something must be done.
- I'd love to see Joshua call his leaders together on the threshold of the Promised Land and say, "Pass the word . . ."
- I'd love to see Nehemiah, having fasted and prayed for four months, risk his life by asking for the king's favor.

There's a time to dream and a time to prepare. But none of that succeeds without decisive action. LifeVesting calls for a different kind of action than many of us are used to. We act *now* for increased returns *later*.

Farmers get the concept. That's why so many life lessons in scripture come from the world of agriculture. To produce a harvest at a set time, we must plant seeds at a set time. To produce an abundant harvest, we must plant abundantly.

Plant Abundantly!
Where Execution Meets Abundance

Sometimes when the Lord wants to tell me something significant, He opens my eyes. Sometimes He literally closes them and speaks to me through a dream. A few years ago I was on an airplane, reading about how God reveals Himself through dreams. I decided to see if the Lord had anything to say to me in that manner. That night in the hotel room, I asked Him to speak to me through my dreams, and I "instructed" my brain to remember.

Remember I did. It was clear, vivid, and unforgettable. I was in the back of one of those big military convoy trucks, along with a couple of other people. I don't remember who they were; they were to my side, helping. Huge sacks of grass seed stood between the tailgate and us. The truck was moving very slowly, and we were dumping grass seed off the back as fast as we could. In my dream I saw the grass come up to full size before my eyes. It was long in some places, short in others. Not your beautifully manicured lawn, but lush, thick, and green. It was abundant.

The next morning I spent some time with the Lord, asking Him what that could mean. As I processed all this in my journal, here is what I sensed Him saying:

> *I have a life and work of abundant fruitfulness for you. Your harvest may not appear as manicured as others. But you will see far more of a harvest if you follow My plan than you ever would if you follow your own. I have given you the capacity to be a harvester and to sow seeds of life, truth, and spiritual power. The opinion of others does not define who you are or what you are called to do. Regardless of your position, you are to be a sower of seed, and you need to sow abundantly. If you do, you will reap abundantly.*

That sure makes sense scripturally. Here's the way Paul put it:

> *He who sows sparingly will also reap sparingly, and he who sows bountifully will also reap bountifully . . . And God is able to make all grace abound to you, so that always having all sufficiency in everything, you may have an abundance for every good deed.*
> 2 Corinthians 9:6, 8

What if you were in the back of that truck, and the "seed" was actually God's love? How much would you plant? What if the seed was forgiveness? Or patience? What if the seed was the good news about Jesus Christ? What if it was money to feed and clothe some child somewhere who didn't have either? What if the seed was laughter and joy? What if it was *yourself*, and your own development? Regardless of the content of the sacks, the message is consistent. Plant sparingly, harvest sparingly. Plant abundantly, then look out!

> *"The kingdom of God is like this," He said. "A man scatters seed on the ground; he sleeps and rises—night and day, and the seed sprouts and grows—he doesn't know how. The soil produces a crop by itself—first the blade, then the head, and then the ripe grain on the head. But as soon as the crop is ready, he sends for the sickle, because harvest has come."*
>
> Mark 4:26–29, HCSB

Buried in the soil, in places no one can see for a while, the seed grows. The same is true for the many ways you can invest in your own life, the lives of others, or the kingdom. Quietly working, sometimes for long seasons, the transformation is happening. Don't assume that just because you can't see visible evidence of results, no results are taking place. It's normal for seeds to grow. It's expected. Why do we act so surprised, then, when we plant a few good things and actually see results?

Don't be deceived into thinking that seeds grow for other people but not for you. You will reap *what* you sow *in proportion* to the amount you've sown. You don't have to manufacture it. You just have to be a faithful participant in the process.

My wife understands the potential of this. On December 26, 2004, she was horrified by news reports from Sri Lanka, Indonesia, and Thailand. To most Americans, this was sad news of a foreign land. To Robin, this was a devastating shock from home. To this day she gives it a proper name: Tsunami.

From ages three to fifteen, Robin Willis grew up in Thailand, the third daughter of medical missionaries. While her parents struggled in language school, she learned to speak Thai from the kids on the street.

The family left the Land of Smiles in 1974 and moved to Texas. Each of them returned on occasion; my father-in-law has gone back many times. All except Robin. It was her dream for years to take our children and me to the place of her childhood. But when the reports of the tsunami devastation came in, Robin knew her time had come. And this would be no vacation.

Foreign relief agencies, individuals, and local businesses began to rise to the occasion. But Robin had a mission of her own. Her father was still licensed to practice medicine in Thailand, so he wasn't confined to a Red Cross tent. Robin organized a medical relief team of doctors, nurses, and support personnel. She contacted local news organizations to publicize the need for medical supplies. Later she raised support for people to rebuild homes and buy fishing boats.

It was incredible to watch how the Lord began preparing her for this journey. She began *dreaming* in Thai! She hadn't spoken the language fluently in over thirty years, but as soon as her feet touched the ground in Bangkok, she regained the language of her past. Memories and experiences of a forgotten childhood flooded her mind and heart. She was home again.

The team focused on three fishing villages, away from the tourist spots so exposed by the media. There they found—even six weeks later—people who had yet to cry. Who clung to pictures of lost family members. Who panicked and fled to high ground when a strong breeze began to blow off the ocean. They found people who had lost every material possession and means of livelihood. It was overwhelming—more than anyone should have to handle. But one day at a time, Robin and the rest of the team reached out and served. Professionals and volunteers executing a plan, abundantly planting God's love. It wasn't just the ten-day trip though. Since then, they have raised thousands of dollars to help buy fishing boats and rebuild homes.

And there was a harvest. By Thai mission standards, a huge one. In a culture that's slow to respond to the gospel, twenty-eight people became followers of Christ while the team was there. Scores more have come to Christ in that area, and people are much more open to the gospel since then. Since somebody decided to plant abundantly.

It doesn't have to be dramatic or a crisis for you to abundantly plant. It just has to be, well, *you*. Believing. Sometimes working alongside others. Sometimes in tears. But offering your time, talent, and treasure to make a difference. Rest assured, you will *doubtless* return with a harvest.

But what if the call to action takes you to unprecedented places? What if you try the impossible or risk the ridiculous? More on that in the next section.

SEED MONEY

1. Read 2 Corinthians 9:1–15. How does God participate in the giving and receiving cycle? What is His role? What is yours? How do you determine your level of participation in this cycle?

2. "I have given you the capacity to be a harvester and to sow seeds of life, truth, and spiritual power. The opinion of others does not define who you are or what you are called to do. Regardless of your position, you are to be a sower of seed, and you need to sow abundantly. If you do, you will reap abundantly." How do these words resonate with you? How might you allow the opinions of others to frame your expectations and actions, rather than the gifts and calling of God on your life?

3. Where are some areas where you sense a need to "plant abundantly"?

4. What specific action can you take this week to plant abundantly in the direction of your vision?

Get Out of the Boat!

Where Execution Meets Leadership

There's a 92 percent chance that nobody will ever criticize you for playing it safe. That's my totally unscientific estimate.

Eleven out of twelve people agree: when all hell's breaking loose, avoid diving into something even more stressful.

What are the odds you would ever be asked to do something completely unprecedented? Electrifyingly dangerous? Humanly impossible? Try 8 percent.

So you can just skip this section and resume your normal activities.

Unless . . .

Unless today's that one-in-twelve—or once-in-a-lifetime—day.

Every investor knows that greater returns require greater risks. That works in kingdom life too. Executing a LifeVesting plan will eventually call you out of the familiar and the "safe." And to influence current or future generations, you'll have to be willing to make the first move.

When was the last time you did something you've always wanted to do but never had the opportunity? Or never had enough time, money, education, help, guts, instructions, or encouragement? When was the last time you tried something new, even at the risk of failure or ridicule? When was the last time you planted a tree, started a business, painted a picture, wrote or told a story? Or climbed a mountain, picked up a new skill, went back to school, or did something *different*? Life is not a spectator sport. Influence and legacies aren't the stuff of armchair quarterbacks and couch potatoes.

One guy in the New Testament is proof of that. He had a habit of making people laugh and creating a stir just by getting up and doing something, or saying something, unafraid of being wrong. And laugh we have. How could anybody be so consistently wrong?

Yep, I'm talking about Peter. Impetuous, clumsy, passionate Peter. A fisherman with a sword (go figure) who charged a mob that was there to arrest Jesus (see John 18:10–11). A natural spokesman who would even argue with or offer advice to Jesus. A guy who would charge headlong into a grave-cave to check things out (see John 20:6). Who would boldly stand and preach Jesus when days earlier he'd been a public spectacle and failure.

My favorite Peter episode took place at night on a stormy sea (see Matthew 14:22–33). There a group of men who navigated boats for a living were terrified. They faced what they believed was their last, and worst, storm ever.

Jesus had insisted they go on without Him while He stayed back to pray. Suddenly, waves crashing and hands full of runaway boat, they saw something even more frightening.

A massive wave? Nope.

Water spout? Negatory.

They saw a ghost.

Seriously? They'd been on a recent miracle-working mission trip. They saw

Jesus feed 5,000 people. And the best they could come with was "It's a ghost!"?

Then—get this—Jesus tells them to be fearless. "Relax!" He said. "It is I."

Great. A *talking* ghost.

Jesus? Couldn't be. I know He works miracles, but it can't be Him. We're on water, He's on land. No, it makes much more sense to assume this is a ghost.

Oh. It *is* Jesus! Whew! I feel better already.

Apparently Peter didn't.

TWO VISIONS OF FOLLOWING JESUS

Yearning to enter the world of the supernatural, not content to cling to the mast for the rest of his life, Peter got this crazy idea in his head.

He did that often.

In fact, Peter always seemed to have this crazy way of thinking, "If Jesus can do it, why can't I?" After all, Jesus *did* say, "Follow me." And Peter had. He followed Jesus and became an instrument of healing and deliverance in His name. He followed Jesus into a challenge to feed 5,000 people. And now? Yet another unprecedented scene. Yet another unscripted adventure.

On that stormy sea, in the boat were two different visions of following Jesus. Neither was *necessarily* right or wrong. But they were very different.

One vision—the super-majority view—was to play it safe. Stay in the boat and attend to business as best you can. Jesus will rescue you from danger and reward you for tending to your boat management duties.

Even James and John—the "Sons of Thunder"—took this approach. And I'll guarantee you they weren't huddled in the hull of the ship, crying like little schoolgirls. They manned their posts—laboring with all their might to get the ship to safety.

And that's the key word in times of peril. Right? The number-one need in this situation is for *safety*.

But wait. There was a minority report. A completely different way of seeing the same situation. Peter, hearing the voice of Jesus, wasn't content with words. He wanted in on the action.

If Jesus can do it, why can't I?

Having the courage and fortitude nobody else had, Peter blurted out, "Lord, if it's really you, tell me to come to you, walking on the water" (Matthew 14:28, NLT).

Crazy! This was the kind of thing you do on *calm* seas, from an *anchored* boat, in *shallow* water. That way you can learn proper water-walking techniques.

That's how 92 percent of the crowd would see it.

Not Peter.

And Jesus met that sense of curiosity, wonder, and I-want-in right where it was. "Come on," He said, and the adventure was on.

Peter jumped over the edge. And walked. On water. Until he took his eyes off Jesus. Then down he went, into the soup.

Was Peter afraid? Of course. But could he refuse his fears and try something completely unprecedented to move toward Jesus?

That's the issue we all face. *Will you keep moving toward Jesus even when you're the only one doing it? Even when it looks insanely impossible? Even when you're terrified?*

The other eleven? They played it safe, huddled in their sinking boat, afraid of the ghost. Most of us wouldn't even be in the boat. We'd watch about it on the Discovery Channel. Have you ever wondered why you never hear anything about James the Lesser? Or Thaddeus or Simon the Zealot, other than in general lists of the disciples? Maybe it's because they never got out of the boat.

WHAT IT MEANS TO GET OUT OF THE BOAT

It means recognizing that where there is no fear, there is no adventure. Where there's no risk of failure, there's no opportunity for rapid growth. Without resisting the storms, there's no opportunity to experience supernatural power.

It means you can trust Jesus in the places and choices where you're most afraid. *Even when you leave your last source of human security, He's worthy of your trust.*

Anybody can play it safe. And in your personal version of Hurricane Katrina or 9/11, nobody would ever criticize you for doing that. Play the odds. Stay with the majority. Opt for safety. You'll be OK.

But maybe this time the call from Jesus is to run *into* the burning building or hurl yourself against the storm. Maybe it's to do something you've never done before—that nobody's done before. Maybe the call from Jesus this time is to join Him and walk on the water.

Get out of the boat! Go to the mission field, even if it's for two weeks. Dare to start that new business or take that job offer. Invite a very poor—or very rich—person to dinner. Adopt a child or sponsor one in another country. Give a whole week's paycheck to a worthy cause. Invite some famous person to speak at your next meeting. Call an old friend and say you miss them or you're sorry. Whether future generations laugh at you or laud you, they'll never even *look* at you until you get up and do something.

Executing your plan takes resources. It takes time, energy, relationships, and money. It also takes timing and wisdom to make the most of every opportunity.

How can you be ready to act when the right time comes? By making the most of the opportunities you have today. In the next section we explore ways you can be intentional and maximize your resources.

SEED MONEY

1. Read Matthew 14:22–33. Why does it seem so hard to believe God immediately after we have seen Him do something amazing? Other than the obvious, what do you think Jesus meant by His question to Peter: "Why did you doubt?" What should Peter have believed? What does that suggest to you about your faith?

2. What would you do or try to do immediately if you knew that you wouldn't be criticized or embarrassed? What does that tell you about the power that others have over your life?

3. "Life is not a spectator sport. Leadership and legacies aren't the stuff of armchair quarterbacks and couch potatoes." What's the first thing that comes to mind when you complete the following sentence? One day, if God will let me, I'm going to _____. Write out what you will do and how you'll do it.

4. What is the first step toward the vision you just wrote down? When and how will you do that this week?

The Life Maximizer

Where Execution Meets Increase

Whatever happened to Green Stamps? They're an indelible memory of my childhood. In case you missed it, Green Stamps were twentieth-century loyalty points. The Sperry & Hutchinson Company began offering stamps to retailers back in 1896. Grocery stores, gas stations, and the like bought the stamps from S&H and gave them as bonuses with every sale. In their heyday, 80 percent of US households collected some kind of stamp.

My sister and I grew up licking green stamps and pasting them in books. When the A&P bag began filling up with completed books, we started getting excited. We'd peer at the two pages of toys in the S&H catalogue. Forget the pages and pages of sheets, clocks, toasters, and other boring things. Truth be told, you could get virtually anything with stamps. A school in Erie, Pennsylvania, exchanged 5.4 million stamps for two gorillas for the local zoo.

Anyway, when we had collected enough to make the trade, we'd go off to the Redemption Center. Technically, we'd already "bought" the stuff. We were presenting evidence of our purchase (the stamps) to redeem—to buy back—our merchandise. Had the stamp books remained in my mother's closet, we would have lived below our privilege. We would have had the *evidence* but not the *experience*.

This section is not about Green Stamps but about redeeming. About buying back something that already belongs to you. If you're going to execute your plan well, you must make the most of your *opportunities* and your *time*.

Two New Testament verses speak to this. Paul says to the Colossians:

> Use your heads as you live and work among outsiders. Don't miss a trick. Make the most of every opportunity.
>
> Colossians 4:5, MSG

To the Ephesians, he said this:

> See then that you walk circumspectly, not as fools but as wise, redeeming the time, because the days are evil.
>
> Ephesians 5:15–16, NKJV

Paul sent both of these messages from prison, of all places! You'd think he had nothing there but time and no opportunities. But even in prison he'd become an expert at seizing his opportunities and buying back the minutes. Paul had won quite a few members of "Caesar's household" to faith in Christ (see Philippians 4:22). So what's your excuse?

Many people in the Bible jumped at what appeared to be an opportunity, only to get bit in the booty by bad timing. Sarah hatched (no pun intended) a plan to help her husband be a dad. Joseph prematurely shared his dreams with a less-than-amused family. Moses "offed" the Egyptian and tried to play referee before his time. The children of Israel tried to storm Canaan after God told them they'd be on the forty-year camper plan. But when the opportunity did arise, in every single case, it came quickly. They were literally making up for lost time.

How about you? Will you be ready when God says, "Go?" When the iron is hot, will you know how, where, and how long to strike?

No. Not without a plan and a prepared heart.

In each of the cases above, God carried His dreamers and leaders through a season of waiting.

Thinking.

Yes, regretting some.

But conceptualizing.

Designing.

Preparing to get it right next time.

So when God named Joshua to succeed Moses, this warrior-turned-statesman was ready. He electrified the crowd with this memo:

> *"Pack your bags. In three days you will cross this Jordan River to enter and take the land GOD, your God, is giving you to possess."*
> Joshua 1:11, MSG

Know why people miss opportunities? Sometimes it's because they're look-ing for opportunities. (I could tell you how I know that, but it's a little embarrassing.) They're lounging on This Ain't My Fantasy Island, waiting for the *SS Opportunity* to chug by.

If you wait to redeem the time until you see the opportunity, you'll never see the opportunity. And you'll waste your life!

If you don't learn to maximize your time and resources when God says, "Wait," you'll never be prepared when God says, "Go." You need a Life Maximizer. Until you shape one of your own, you can borrow mine.

MAKING THE MOST OF THE DAY

Remember those three lists I told you about? I wasn't content to itemize them. I wanted to learn from them. I wanted to learn how to redesign my life before God so that when opportunities arose I could take quick action. For me that meant creating a tool to help channel my thinking and actions in the right direction. I began thinking of it as my own personalized planner. I learned from my lists about the things that mattered most to me and looked for a way to plan around them. I focused on the states of mind and heart I wanted to experience each day. I learned from the life of Joseph. If I cultivated faithfulness in the daily spaces and dark places, one day the prison doors would open. And opportunity would come calling (see Genesis 40-41).

So, beginning with the end of the day in mind, I asked myself, "At the end of the perfect day *for me,* what can I say that I have done?" Here is what that looks like for me. Your answer to the question, of course, would be your own.

At the end of the perfect day, I have *connected* with God, myself, and other people. I have *created* something of value by thinking, imagining, worshipping. I have *encouraged* somebody to hang in, move on, stand up, or turn around. I have *energized* my life by the right food, rest, or exercise. I have *expressed* love, commitment, passion, or enthusiasm. I have *grown* spiritually, mentally, relationally. And I have *produced* by moving a step or two closer to a goal.

From that I made myself a planning tool—I call it my Daily Life Maximizer. When I use it, I plan by the week but work it by the day. For each day of the week, in a context of prayer and seeking the Lord, I give myself the following challenges. Then I ask the corresponding empowering questions:

Connect

What can I do today to reach up toward God, reach out toward people, and reach in to connect with myself? This involves five things:

1. Giving/receiving praise
2. Giving/receiving gratitude
3. Identifying/confessing mistakes, sins, or wrongs
4. Asking for/receiving help
5. Protecting, honoring, or staying loyal

How can I express that in all my relationships today?

Create

What can I do today to create value through music, writing, art, drama, or some other form of original thought?

Encourage

What can I do today to encourage another human being? Who needs a letter written, a gift received, a call or visit? Who needs to "feel" I am "walking with them" through their pain or joy? Who needs to be motivated to hang in, move on, stand up, or turn around? Who needs helpful and wanted advice?

Energize

What can I do today to increase my energy level—either by food, rest, or exercise?

Express

What can I do today to express enthusiasm, passion, love, or commitment to the things and people who matter to me?

Grow

What can I do today to expand my knowledge, experience, or character? What can I read or study? How can I spend time with instructional people?

Produce

What major step can I accomplish today toward a goal or project?

If you want, use my Life Maximizer. Better still, ask God for wisdom to create your own. Ask empowering questions and you'll get powerful answers. When you learn to maximize the time, you'll also find God entrusting to you His opportunities.

Keep in mind that LifeVesting is a *growth* process. As you maximize your time and opportunities, you'll find your character being stretched. If opportunity comes to the prepared heart, how does God prepare yours for what's coming? That's the subject of the next section.

SEED MONEY

1. Read Joshua 1:1–9. How did God prepare Joshua to lead the Israelites into quick and decisive action?

2. "At the end of the perfect day *for me,* what can I say that I have done?" Describe the perfect day for you.

3. What are some things that hinder or distract you from achieving your perfect day?

4. Design your own Life Maximizer. Based on your "perfect day" answers, design some questions to ask yourself weekly or daily. How can you make the most of your time and life?

Freedom through Surrender
Where Execution Meets Freedom

Inside you lies a deep desire. It's quiet but compelling. It's one of the secrets of what motivates you—in fact, your deep, abiding happiness depends on it. Yet it's hidden. So behind-the-scenes, if I were to ask you to list your strongest longings, this wouldn't make the list. But it's there. It's powerful. And your response to it may be the difference between addicted and sober. Between ambition and actualization. Between frustration and fulfillment.

The desire? You want to inherit the earth. And you want it badly.

You can trace that desire all the way back to the first man. After all, it's why we were placed on this planet in the first place. "Fill the earth and subdue it," God said (Genesis 1:28, NIV). You were made to manage. To be large and in charge, beginning with your own life. Jesus said that those who inherit the earth are deeply satisfied, genuinely happy (see Matthew 5:5). But something has gone terribly wrong. As humans we're not particularly happy. I'm not so sure we're inheriting the earth either.

WHAT, EXACTLY, DOES THAT MEAN?

David also talked about inheriting the earth in Psalm 37 and gave some hints about what it means.

> *Trust in the LORD, and do good;*
> *Dwell in the land, and feed on His faithfulness.*
> *Delight yourself also in the LORD,*
> *And He shall give you the desires of your heart. . . .*
> *But the meek shall inherit the earth,*
> *And shall delight themselves in the abundance of peace.*
>
> Psalm 37:3–4, 11

Those who inherit the earth have all their needs met. Figuratively speaking, they "feed on God's faithfulness." Inheriting the earth means enjoying abundant peace and prosperity. That is, having your needs and desires fulfilled without conflict or insecurity.

You were made for that.

You want that.

Your happiness depends on it.

SO WHY NOT JUST GO GET IT?

The problem we have isn't the desire. It's human to want abundant peace and prosperity. The problem is what we do to try to get it, and how we demand to have it *now*. Conventional wisdom says, "If you want it, grab it." The logical approach is to achieve through ambition. Simply do all the mental and relational things the world tells us to do to get what we want.

But those who inherit the earth don't do so by *capturing* it. Not that we haven't tried. The study of history is usually organized around a timeline of would-be world conquerors. No, you get the earth by inheriting it. That implies several things, starting with the passage of (sometimes a lot of) time. Add to that a relationship to the One giving the inheritance. Then a gift that comes through that relationship.

Do you realize how many people are in bondage because they couldn't wait to get what they wanted? Maybe it's emotional bondage to a dead-end relationship, or to something that offered a quick solution to pain. Maybe it's financial bondage that couldn't see past a sale and a credit card. Each of these is driven by ambition (desire) void of a relationship with the One who owns it all in the first place. "The earth is the LORD's, and all it contains" (Psalm 24:1). If we so deeply want and need to inherit the earth, doesn't it make sense to pursue a trust relationship with the One who owns it?

There is a subtler, more sinister form of ambition. It's the ambition of *possessing*. How often do we clutch something that was intended for our benefit but not our possession? This kind of ambition takes place whenever we try to package the gifts and blessings God gives us. It happened on the Mount of Transfiguration, where Peter suggested they package the spectacle in three tents (see Matthew 17:4). It happens in our lives when we selfishly try to clutch or own something that feels like it adds value to our lives. Maybe it's the heart of a beloved or the obedient affection of a child. Maybe it's the dying breath of a parent or the job or the career we have always loved and longed for. God gives it to bless us. But we cling to it, and as a result, we cross lines and create idols. We make demands, and our heart darkens.

It even happens in our relationship with God—what the preachers refer to as loving the gift more than the Giver. I've seen it happen often in my own life. After praying, seeking, knocking on God's door, He comes through. I'm so excited, so grateful. And so human! My next thought is like that of a spoiled child: "Oh God, would You do that again please?" Or like Peter: "Lord, let's build a tent around this, so I can come back for another dose whenever I want it or need it!" We also try to systematize whatever we did before we experienced that blessing so we can receive it again. We pray the same prayer or follow the same steps. We develop systems for God. And when these systems fail us, as all systems do, we blame God.

There is another way. It's the way of *meekness*. The meek inherit the earth. And then they go on being meek. And go on inheriting the earth.

The meek don't inherit the earth so they can say, "Good! Now I don't have to be meek anymore." When they taste some of the fruits of their inheritance, they're grateful, but they don't get attached to it. They remain detached. They hold things loosely. They remain watchful. Wonder-full. Sensitive to the Spirit's quiet promptings.

SO HE RESERVES IT FOR SISSIES?

Not exactly. As the old saying goes, "Meekness is not weakness. It's strength under control." The word Jesus used for *meek* or *gentle* referred to a colt that had been broken. A gentle horse is not a weak horse, but one that has submitted its strength to the will of its rider. Meekness is the result of a training process that God takes us through in stages.

Stage 1: Submission to the Master's will
Here you come to the complete surrender of your will to God's.

Stage 2: Receiving the Master's training
Meekness means having a teachable spirit. That involves letting God condition you and apply what you've learned.

Stage 3: Enduring the Master's testing

All meekness is tested. In Psalm 37 you can find four tests of meekness.

> *Do not fret because of evildoers,*
> *Nor be envious of the workers of iniquity.*
>
> Psalm 37:1, NKJV

The test of *anxiousness*. What are you going to do when the Lord has told you to do something, and He doesn't seem to be coming through?

The test of *envy*. What will you do when you're doing what you think is right, yet those who live sinful lives get more blessing?

> *Cease from anger, and forsake wrath;*
> *Do not fret—it only causes harm.*
>
> Psalm 37:8, NKJV

The test of *anger*. What will you do when someone violates your "rights"?

The test of *retaliation*. What will you do when someone offends you, hurts you, or does something wrong to you?

In any test, there's only one meek answer . . .

Stage 4: Obeying the Master's voice

Meekness means learning to respond quickly when God speaks. You'll have to harness the strength God has given you to make that happen. Moses, for example, was referred to as the meekest man in Israel (see Numbers 12:3). He defied the mightiest king on earth but endured fierce criticism without retaliation. David stood before Goliath with fire in his eyes. But when he had an opportunity to kill Saul, he refused to stretch out his hand against God's anointed. Jesus Himself stilled raging storms, but "when he was reviled, reviled not again" (1 Peter 2:23, KJV).

That's meekness. Not the stuff of sissies and wimps. Just the character of the believer who has learned to fulfill his deepest longings through surrender.

In the natural, executing your plan means harnessing your own energy to push through a plan. Not so in LifeVesting. LifeVestors learn to listen to an inner voice. It speaks first to your character, then to your plans. Learn to hear and respond to that voice of His Spirit, and it will lead you to freedom and fulfillment of your deepest desires.

So what's He telling you?

Executing a plan in God's kingdom begins with marshaling the power of God to bear on your situation. As Watchman Nee once wrote, "He who is powerless before God is powerless before men." In the next section we explore the response of Jesus to the most profound of requests: "Lord, teach us to pray."

SEED MONEY

1. Read 1 Peter 2:20–25. How is Jesus an example of meekness? How does this example apply to your life?

2. "Do you realize how many people are in bondage because they couldn't wait to get what they wanted?" Could that be you? What do you have a hard time waiting for, or giving God time to finish?

3. Based on the four tests from Psalm 37, how is your meekness being tested these days?

4. 4. What can you do to increase your capacity to hear God's voice and respond to His leading?

Keep Knocking!
Where Execution Meets Eternity

On September 16, 2001, an amazing phenomenon took place. In churches across the United States, civilians came out of their foxholes. And in the wake of the terrorist attacks, they were talking about God. On that day, in American churches everywhere, people came looking for answers.

Within a matter of weeks, however, things had settled down to business as usual. The *Washington Times* later predicted a change in the nation's spiritual landscape. Within a decade, they said, Americans would "invent" a religion of their own that met their needs. Why? When they revisited the places that had once nourished them, they didn't find what they were looking for. To be fair, they may have been looking for a place that let them have a god of their own making.

The fact that people may try to invent a religion of their own doesn't bother me—we've been doing that since Adam and Eve. What bothers me is that when they came to our house—the church—looking for answers, something was missing.

What if they came to our house looking for answers, and we were as confused as they were? What if they came looking for life, and we were just as dead? What if they came looking for power, yet all they found was platitudes, programs, and politics?

Our greatest teaching opportunities often arise when we recognize something is missing. Remember when the disciples couldn't cast a demon out of a boy, and they asked Jesus why (see Matthew 17:19)? That was a teachable moment.

Another one took place after Jesus had sent them out on their first mission excursion. They came back excited about people saved, healed, and delivered. Yet still they recognized something was missing. They saw the difference between how Jesus prayed and how they did. They remembered what He said, "The harvest is so great, and the workers are so few. So *pray* . . ." (Matthew 9:37–38, TLB).

They got it. So they came to Him with a simple request: "Lord, teach us to pray" (Luke 11:1). It's the greatest investment you can make in eternity.

DEPENDENCE

The first thing Jesus did in response to their request was to give them an example of what to say. We call it the Model Prayer (see Luke 11:2–4). It has five parts: praise, submission, petition, confession, and protection. It's remarkable in its simplicity and directness. Jesus never intended it to be a vain repetition but a guide for the things to talk to God about.

Approach Him as Father, but a Father whose name is holy.

Approach Him with the recognition that His kingdom is where our citizenship remains. But as long as we have breath on this earth, we will live in the tension between His kingdom and the world's.

Approach Him with needs, big and small.

Approach Him with your guilt and conflicts, and release both into His hands.

Approach Him with your vulnerability to temptation and ask for His help.

In each of these things you ask God to do what only God can do. You declare again your need for and dependence on Him. Praying reestablishes your reliance on God and reminds you that He's God and you're not.

Christians lose power in their walk with God when they make the Christian life a "do it yourself" project. Many of us get saved and assume the rest is up to us. God is calling His church back to an understanding that all the power we ever need is available to us—but it isn't our power!

PERSISTENCE

Jesus dropped a startling truth on the guys by telling them a story:

> *"Suppose you went to a friend's house at midnight, wanting to borrow three loaves of bread. You would shout up to him, 'A friend of mine has just arrived for a visit and I've nothing to give him to eat.' He would call down from his bedroom, 'Please don't ask me to get up. The door is locked for the night and we are all in bed. I just can't help you this time.'*
>
> *"But I'll tell you this—though he won't do it as a friend, if you keep knocking long enough, he will get up and give you everything you want—just because of your persistence."*
>
> Luke 11:5–8, TLB

Get what Jesus is saying here. In prayer, *persistence is more powerful than friendship or relationship*. With all the Bible's emphasis on a relationship with God, this is an amazing statement. God will respond even more to your persistence in calling on Him than He will respond to you out of love.

The word translated *persistence* means "shameless." The idea is that we're not put to shame if God doesn't respond to our request the first time. We don't fret about bothering God; we just keep asking. If that doesn't get a response, we keep seeking. If that doesn't get a response, we keep knocking.

The reason some of us lose spiritual power is that we become discouraged. We ask and don't get an answer, so we give up. But your heavenly Father is waiting for some shameless asking, seeking, and knocking!

PERSPECTIVE

> *"You fathers—if your children ask for a fish, do you give them a snake instead? Or if they ask for an egg, do you give them a scorpion? Of course not! So if you sinful people know how to give good gifts to your children, how much more will your heavenly Father give the Holy Spirit to those who ask him."*
>
> Luke 11:11–13, NLT

Our attitude matters. We must approach God as one who knows how to give good gifts to His children. The enemy tries to sell the lie that God is the kind of Father who gives us snakes when we ask for fish. But God not only responds to our requests as requests; He responds to them by personally getting involved in our lives. The Holy Spirit is God, and He is God's personal answer to our needs, petitions, requests, and dreams.

Every time I ask in faith for a simple request, my heavenly Father responds by giving Himself first. And when He gives me the Holy Spirit as the answer, one of three things will happen: (1) I receive the supernatural answer I'm asking for; (2) I receive "exceeding abundantly" more; or (3) I receive something in His presence that makes the original request meaningless.

Every child instinctively knows this. Have you noticed that when they ask a parent to do something, what they want most often is the parent, not the request? When my twins were small, it wasn't the glass of water they wanted after the lights were out. It wasn't the stories I sometimes told. It was me. They trusted me. They wanted my presence.

One early morning, the Lord literally gave me a message in a dream—something that had never happened to me before. Here's what He said:

"My people are powerless because deep down inside,
they think that if they ask for a fish, I'm going to give them a snake."

Maybe it's disappointment. Maybe it's fear. Maybe it's guilt, or maybe it's anger. But something has led you to question whether you can trust your Father. God's answer to you is, yes, you can.

LifeVestors invest in eternity by taking massive action. On their knees. It's time for a new Declaration of Dependence. Some shameless knocking on heaven's door. And simple trust that your Father cares enough to get personally involved.

If the plan is big enough to act on, it's big enough for you to call on Him.

SEED MONEY

1. Read Luke 11:1–13. What promises does Jesus make to you in these verses?

2. What is the difference between asking, seeking, and knocking? What are you asking God for, seeking God for, and knocking on God's door for right now?

3. "My people are powerless because deep down inside, they think that if they ask for a fish, I'm going to give them a snake." Do you have difficulty trusting God for things you may feel you don't deserve? Explain.

4. For encouragement purposes, start a diary of answered prayer. Practice here. Give a brief account of two or three answered prayers you have received lately. When did you start praying, what did you ask God to do, and how and when did He answer you? If you can't recall any answered prayer, write out what you're asking God to do for you.

FINAL THOUGHT

Back to that list I started at the beginning of this chapter. There's a pattern to it, of course. I want to see what makes people risk making the first move.

History always judges its successes and failures. But the linchpin to every meaningful change was a decision to move forward. To dare. To dream. To try.

You can make history too. But nobody ever made history as a spectator.

Execute!

CHAPTER 6

Protect Your Investment

L et me tell you about the time I tried to climb a tree.

In a car.

I didn't succeed.

I walked away (literally), and neither the car nor the tree was amused.

Early 90s. I was making the little run from my house to the office—something I did every day. In between one neighborhood and another was a half-mile woodsy, country stretch.

And there was this little ditch.

I'd never noticed it before. But you can bet I never ignored it again. The ditch was just wide enough for my right tires to slip in. And slip they did. At 30 miles per hour my wheels dropped into the ditch as if I were in an oversized slot car.

I should point out here that my car, like most cars, had two pedals. But I always figured the big one was mostly for decoration. So I didn't hit the brakes—I just tried to wheel my way back out of the ditch.

That wasn't happening.

What *was* happening was the sudden appearance of a massive oak tree. The thought never occurred to me to hit the brakes. So I wound up ramming my car into the tree and fender-climbing it a bit.

Nothing hurt but my pride. And the car, which I never drove again.

This real-life experience became a metaphor for what can often happen in life. I've seen it happen to people's careers. Their influence. Their relationships. Their personal lives at whatever level. Somewhere, somehow, without wanting to, they hit the ditch. They're stuck. Powerless. A bit wrecked or hurt and halfway up a tree. Without help, they're going nowhere.

Nobody sets out to wreck their lives or loves by hitting the ditch. But in a state of mass humanization, it can easily happen to the best of us. That's why it's so important when pursuing life goals to know how to play defense. You must learn to protect your investment. That's the next stage in the LifeVesting cycle.

Dig Your Reservoirs and Gather Your Jars
Where Protection Meets Abundance

It was a poignant conversation that probably ended too quickly. I'm sure it called for more tenderness and empathy than I offered at the time. But hey, at least it was honest.

"I was saved at age six, and Spirit-filled at age nine," she said plaintively. "Now I don't even know if there is a God. How do I get my faith back?"

We were sitting in a church house, which she hadn't seen in a long time. I blurted out an answer that distressed more than blessed. *"You start by showing up."*

I'm sure that wasn't the answer she was looking for, but I still think it's true. She would never "get her faith back" while she avoided the places where blessing and faith are cultivated. Same goes for you.

Often when we think of "protection" we imagine insuring ourselves against misfortune. That drives the whole insurance industry. But LifeVestors also insure themselves *for* blessing. In this section we'll explore how the law of abundance can do more than protect our lives today. It can also prepare us for the blessing God wants to give us tomorrow. We serve a God who can do "far more abundantly beyond all we that we ask or think" (Ephesians 3:20). But He insists that we get involved in the process. It's one thing to pray. It's another to be prepared for the answer.

TWO FAITH-SIZED MIRACLES

This is illustrated in back-to-back stories in 2 Kings 3–4. Two different people summoned the prophet Elisha. The first was the king of Israel, whose army was dehydrated and facing sure defeat. The second was the widow of a prophet, who was facing the loss of her sons to slavery to pay off her creditor.

Elisha advised similar things. To Israel's king he said, "Make this valley full of ditches. You will see neither wind nor rain, yet this valley will be filled with water" (2 Kings 3:17, NIV). To the widow he said, "Go around and ask all your neighbors for empty jars. Don't ask for just a few. . . . Pour oil into all the jars, and as each is filled, put it to one side" (2 Kings 4:3–4, NIV).

How much water did the armies of Israel and Judah receive? As much as the ditches they dug would contain. How much oil did the widow supernaturally receive? As much as she had collected jars to hold. God has His part; we have ours. But God won't fill what our faith hasn't prepared.

HOW PREPARED IS YOUR HORSE?

The horse is prepared for the day of battle,
But victory belongs to the LORD.

Proverbs 21:31

This is another reminder to be faithful to do your part, but to trust God to do His. Your only responsibility is to see to it that the "horse" is prepared for the day of battle.

So what's your "horse"? *Anything that prepares you for a victory only God can provide.* Yes, that means being faithful to plan, to prepare, to execute. Yet God sees to the results.

Here you can fall into two ditches. First, you can fail to prepare the "horse," whatever that may represent. Through negligence or laziness, you can arrive at the day of battle with an unprepared horse.

The other mistake is to try to control the results. You could attempt shortcuts on preparing your horse. Or you could try to do both God's job yours and try to secure the victory by doing it all yourself. But you'd be assuming a load that God never intended you to carry. The result? Unnecessary, deceptive feelings of failure or stress. Or worse, the appearance of results without real spiritual fruit.

Bottom line: God has His part and you have yours. It takes both to live in the fullness of your blessing.

Let me introduce you to a guy with a prepared horse. Bartimaeus was a blind beggar who lived in Jericho (see Mark 10:46–52). He heard an excited crowd passing by one day and discovered it was the entourage surrounding Jesus. He began to holler. Out loud, rowdy, and obnoxious. The more the rabble tried to shut him up, the louder he got. So, Jesus stopped and asked him the golden question:

"What do you want Me to do for you?"

Here was faith that refused to be quiet. This blind man saw clearer than the multitude of sighted people around Jesus. He understood something of Jesus' heart. I wonder if the locals would still have told him to be quiet had they known in advance he would be healed that day.

"What do you want Me to do for you?"

The blind man also understood how desperate his own situation was. He had an affliction he could do nothing about. But he faced an opportunity to meet the only One who could change it. And this man genuinely wanted to be free from blindness.

"What do you want Me to do for you?"

This man understood what mattered most. Notice how he made his living. He was a panhandler, a professional connoisseur of charity. The size of the crowd meant more people who could give money. Yet when he heard that Jesus approached, charity was the furthest thing from his mind.

The more helpless you realize you are, the more you need to trust the heart of Christ. Even if the whole world is telling you to shut up and deal with it. He still frees desperate people from desperate situations. But you still have to do your part. Let go of the vain values that so often hold you captive and consider what truly matters. Imagine the tragedy of the wrong answer to Jesus' question. Can't you just imagine this guy saying, "Could you spare me some change?"

PREPARATION MEETS PROVISION

Things looked bleak for the children in George Muller's orphanage in England. It was time for breakfast at Ashley Downs. They had no food in the kitchen and no money in the bank. The young daughter of a close friend of Muller's was visiting in the home. The great man of faith took her hand and said, "Come and see what our Father will do."

In the dining room, long tables were set with empty plates and empty mugs. Muller prayed, "Dear Father, we thank You for what You are going to give us to eat." Immediately they heard a knock at the door; there stood the local baker. "Mr. Muller," he said, "I couldn't sleep last night. Somehow I felt you had no bread for breakfast, so I got up at 2:00 this morning and baked fresh bread. Here it is."

Muller thanked him and gave praise to God. Soon he heard a second knock—the milkman. His cart had broken down in front of the orphanage. He wanted to give the children the milk so he could empty the cart and repair it. I guess it was a good thing they had plates and mugs ready.

I've met Christians who blame God for a raw deal. They ask for healing and don't get it. But they haven't dug a ditch into their unhealthy lifestyle or belief system big enough to contain the healing that the Lord could provide. Is that always the reason we pray for healing and don't get it? By no means. But it's worth asking, have I adjusted my life to the desired outcome?

Others ask God to restore a broken relationship. But they haven't prepared a heart big enough to hold that restored relationship. Still others have financial pressure and want God to increase their cash flow. But they haven't taken the time to learn God's ways of managing the resources they already have. With our words we say, "Come in," but with our actions or unbelief we say, "Stay out." Somehow, though, it's always God's fault.

If you're needing big and praying big, you'd better be hauling out a big container. Our God is all-powerful, but He's also a gentleman. He can change whatever He enters, but He only enters wherever He's welcome. Where is He asking you to trust Him? How is He asking you to obey Him? How are you preparing for the blessing to follow? If you're holding out a thimble, don't ask for the ocean.

SEED MONEY

1. Read Ephesians 3:14–21. If someone were praying this for you, what would it look like if God answered the prayer? How would you change or grow?

2. What about your disappointments—your apparent "raw deals" from God? Reflect on them. What are they, and how do you feel about them?

3. "If you're needing big, and praying big, you'd better be hauling out a big container." If the Lord were to come through and deliver your greatest desires, what would you have to do to prepare for it?

4. Based on your answer above, what specific thing will you do this week to "dig a deeper reservoir" for God to fill?

Fools at the Finish Line

Where Protection Meets Leadership

I went to the Fred Flintstone School of Golf. Simple philosophy: when in doubt, hit the ball *really hard*; when not in doubt, hit the ball *really hard*. Maybe you've heard that old golf saying—"You drive for show and putt for dough." Suffice it to say, I've never made any money hitting a ball in a hole with a stick. I have, however, put on a show by hitting a ball *off* a stick.

All that's fine and fun when you're dealing with woods and wedges. But life is a different story. A mere proverb in the gentleman's game is brutal reality in the real world:

It's not how you drive but how you arrive.

Not how you start but how you finish. Magilla Gorilla and Fred Flintstone need not apply.

Life is filled with stories of people who started well but crashed out. They could have left a heritage, with inspiring and ennobling footsteps to follow. Instead, their names and stories are relegated to footnotes and tales of warning. Or questions that begin with, "Whatever happened to . . . ?"

Protecting your investment isn't a one-time experience. The blessings we receive and battles we win are part of the journey of a lifetime. Others are following your lead. That's why it's important to identify potential snares that can trip you up or hold you back.

It's up to you. Will you be a driver or an arriver?

I must warn you, if you decide to go the distance, the deck is stacked against you. This is a marathon not a dash. You're surrounded by mediocre runners and a grandstand full of fat critics. But you do have a Coach—the Lord Jesus Himself. Under His direction, you'll learn to identify these six tripping points.

> *Therefore, since we are surrounded by such a great cloud of witnesses, we must get rid of every weight and the sin that clings so closely, and run with endurance the race set out for us, keeping our eyes fixed on Jesus, the pioneer and perfecter of our faith. For the joy set out for him he endured the cross, disregarding its shame, and has taken his seat at the right hand of the throne of God.*
>
> Hebrews 12:1–2, NET

UNNECESSARY WEIGHTS

Runners train by wearing weights on their ankles. But you'd never see a marathoner show up to an actual event with them. Races aren't exactly coat-and-tie affairs either. The goal of the runner is to be light and free. Too bad we often miss that point off the track.

I've known many people who are multitalented but mole-blind to their limitations. And you can add my name to the list! I created a lot of pain for myself and others because in my arrogance, I thought I could handle anything. Extra monthly payment here? No problem. I can handle it. Another time commitment there? Sure, I can handle it. My life at times became like the seed that fell on the thorn-laced ground in Jesus' story. My fruitfulness was choked by competing commitments (see Mark 4:19).

Paul put the dilemma this way:

> *"Everything is permissible," but not everything is beneficial.*
>
> 1 Corinthians 12:23, CSB

You can do anything, but you can't do everything. That's why you have to discern the difference between the good and the best. If you don't choose the essential over the optional, you'll never finish well.

REPEATED FAILURE

To some people, one failure is fatal. They become consumed with guilt and shame. And without a grace awakening they never rise out of the ditch of self-condemnation. There's another ditch, though, that's just as fatal—accepting consistent failure as normal. That's why Hebrews encourages us to "lay aside . . . the sin that clings so closely" (Hebrews 12:1, ESV). Read this carefully:

> *Your worth isn't measured by your performance,*
> *but your* memory is measured *by your* endurance.

Look at Judas. Here was a man just as instrumental in life-changing ministries as James or John. He preached the gospel, healed the sick, cast out demons, and many other things. But nobody remembers that. They only remember his treachery and suicide.

DISTORTED VISION

Competitive runners talk of the importance of maintaining stride. It's easier said than done. It requires focus on a target—a finish line. For Christ followers, our finish line is personal. It's Jesus Himself.

Focus is the downfall for many spiritual "runners." When you look to the grandstands for who's cheering you on instead of looking to Jesus, you'll lose stride. Same goes for when you compare yourself to other runners or look back at where you have been. You lose stride when you gaze at the impossible distance ahead. Ditto for when you focus on your pain, fatigue, or weaknesses. The Christian life is about Jesus, not you, the pack you run in, or the crowds watching you. Focus on Him; it's the only way to maintain stride.

OVERWHELMING RESISTANCE

> *When you find yourselves flagging in your faith, go over that story again, item by item, that long litany of hostility he plowed through. That will shoot adrenaline into your souls!*
>
> Hebrews 12:3, MSG

The world resisted Jesus and will resist you on some level if you follow Him. Many believers found their faith and testimony on the rocks because they felt alone against the crowd and blew it. It's easy to say, like Peter, "Even if everyone else falls to pieces on account of you, I won't" (Matthew 26:33, MSG). But when everybody around you is pushing against the Lord, the easy path goes along to get along. When that happens, you're ripe for epic failure.

You can't avoid the reality of resistance. But you can make sure you don't fight your battles dependent on your own pride and passion.

TOTAL EXHAUSTION

People do stupid things when they're hungry, angry, lonely, or tired. That's why the writer of Hebrews warns us to "not grow weary and lose heart" (12:3, NIV). That warning speaks to us on many levels. Our spiritual, emotional, mental, and physical lives are all vulnerable. Each life dimension requires food, rest, exercise, and care. If you've been running on empty in any of these areas for an extended time, look out for trouble. You face the danger of making impulsive, in-the-moment choices, which can have devastating, long-term consequences. Not one component of your system was made for continuous operation. Even the Lord took a day off.

PERSONAL ISOLATION

The Hebrew Christians were undergoing intense stress. They had lost sight of *God* in the situation (see Hebrews 12:4–7) and become isolated. The truth is, none of us were intended to do anything, for any length of time, alone. Solomon recognized that:

A man who isolates himself seeks his own desire;
He rages against all wise judgment.

Proverbs 18:1, NKJV

Satan's favorite tool to make you tomorrow's byword is to separate you from healthy community. The Bible reads like a who's who of failure-in-isolation. David, Samson, Judas, and Solomon were all powerful when they started. But they all were limping when they finished, if they finished at all.

Finish well. You're in a marathon, and the human odds are against you. But the stakes are high, and the promise of this race is that you never run alone. In the next section, we'll check out someone who finished well and left a trail to follow.

SEED MONEY

1. Read Colossians 3:5–10. Here's another list of things that can weigh you down. Do you see anything there that tends to hinder your effectiveness?

2. "I've known many people who are multitalented but mole-blind to their limitations." How do you reconcile faith for the impossible with wise recognition of your limitations? What are some of your limitations, and how should you respond to them?

3. Six things that undermine believers are mentioned in this section. Which are particularly limiting to you? How should you go about reversing their effects and arming yourself against them?

4. Read Colossians 3:12–17. Based on the issues you have listed in the three previous questions, which of these exhortations will you focus on this week to position you for victory?

The Cat's in the Cradle

Where Protection Meets Increase

He's an old man now. His physical vision is virtually gone; his heartbeat will soon follow. His spiritual vision? That's another story. It's still bright, filled with fire and hope. But that vision now sees through the eyes of other men. He's increasing his influence, but others now carry his banner.

He has no children of his own but does know someone who may as well be. He's one of those blessed individuals who knows his time's up, yet faces eternity with no regrets. And now he writes the man he calls his son in the faith. His future looks bright; he can only pray the same for Tim.

> *Stand steady, and don't be afraid of suffering for the Lord. Bring others to Christ. Leave nothing undone that you ought to do.*
> *I say this because I won't be around to help you very much longer. My time has almost run out. Very soon now I will be on my way to heaven. I have fought long and hard for my Lord, and through it all I have kept true to him. And now the time has come for me to stop fighting and rest.*
> 2 Timothy 4:5–7, TLB

A decade before I became a father myself, Harry Chapin sucker-slapped dads everywhere. His "Cat's in the Cradle" reminded us that catching the plane wasn't as important as catching a baseball with your son. Ending your life with no regrets makes a father wealthier than ending it with no debts.

The song spoke to me as a high school sophomore. As long as I could remember, I'd hoped to have kids of my own. It continues to speak to me now, eleven grandchildren later, deeply wanting to leverage my life. I know I can redeem the time, but I can't relive it.

I look to this old man in prison who has danced with death for years. And for a little while, I'm Timothy. I'm the preacher-boy he believes in. The one in whom he has invested his teaching, his leadership, his life, and now his last recorded words. I gaze at Paul with wonder. How do you do that? How do you maximize every moment so powerfully? How do you avoid so easily the things that seem to push me around at will?

In my mentor's final charge to me I find some specifics to help finish what I started. Six red flags to watch for that Satan uses to tempt me now and torture me later. Now well-armed, alerted, and faithful to follow through, I can invest in my legacy, my eternity, *and* my lifetime. I can finish well.

The message is clear: *Don't screw up.* Anybody can have flash-in-the-pan results. How do we invest our lives so they produce an increase for the long haul and avoid regrets?

UNAWAKE MINDS

> *But you must keep a clear head in everything.*
> 2 Timothy 4:5, GW

That's easier said than done. We live in a world that gladly offers to do our thinking for us. It promises to numb our pain and entertain us while we stand in line for our own funeral. It promises pleasure, prosperity, and the chance to feel good about ourselves. All the world's system asks for in return? Conform. Get in the boat but don't rock it. Don't *think.* Don't challenge. The result? A lifetime of convenience followed by the pitiful refrain: "I never knew . . . "

UN-ENDURED AFFLICTION

> *Accept the hard times along with the good.*
> 2 Timothy 4:5, MSG

Paul never discussed hardship as a possibility. He assumed it would happen. And he made it clear that it wasn't just the devil's idea. Soldiers go to boot camp to learn how to survive in the heat of battle. So also God will take us to spiritual boot camp to prepare us for the really tough times.

I've never met anybody who regretted hanging in there, trying one more time. But I've met plenty who pulled the trap door on a relationship, a career, a job, an idea when it got hard. Then later they wished they could have one more chance to make it work. "What if" is a painful thing to say on your deathbed.

UNREALIZED INFLUENCE

Work at telling others the Good News.

2 Timothy 4:5, NLT

For Paul influencing others wasn't work. His ministry was bold, creative, and consistent. He was an in-your-face leader, and people followed.

Timothy was different. More introverted than his spiritual father, he preferred to let Paul do the talking for him. He was nonconfrontational and passive. Paul had to remind him to rekindle the gifts God had given him (2 Timothy 1:6).

Whether you're a natural or have to work at it, you have your own realm of influence that nobody else can touch. People in that realm will receive *somebody's* view of God. *Somebody's* view of life, love, hope, freedom, relationships, or mission. Will they believe a truth or a lie? Wide road or narrow? It all depends on what you do with the power God gave you to touch them.

UNFULFILLED CALLINGS

Fully carry out the ministry God has given you.

2 Timothy 4:5, NLT

Timothy's calling, like yours and mine, was as unique as a fingerprint or snowflake. But to understand *your* calling, start with *our* calling. You can't identify your *unique* mission until you've committed to the *common* mission. "God's will" is more important than "God's will for my life." The emphasis is not on you. It's not *about* you. It's about the faithful God who calls you and will equip you to fulfill that calling. When you're committed to God's mission, your calling within it will emerge. But it isn't enough to *find* it. You have to *fulfill* it.

UNFOUGHT BATTLES

I have fought the good fight, I have finished the race, I have kept the faith.

2 Timothy 4:7, NKJV

To be successful in any area of life, sooner or later you'll have to fight for it. You'll have to fight for your family; sometimes that means fighting *with* some family member. You will have to fight for your legacy. You'll have to fight for your walk with God. And sometimes, when you run to the battlefield, you may discover you're the only one standing there.

Don't misunderstand. I'm not talking about copying those people who live from one conflict or offense to the next. I'm talking about the spirit of young David. Remember when he confronted his smart-mouthed brothers and took down a trash-talking giant? He had a cause greater than his comfort, convenience, or popularity. So do you! And there's a time to refuse to back down.

UNFINISHED BUSINESS

"I've finished the race," Paul said. This one nails me because of the many pieces of unfinished business I have accumulated in my life. It got so bad, I declared one year "the Year of Unfinished Business." That one-year Bible reading plan I started? Finished it. In fifteen years. The main thing is I got it done.

Why do lives gather up such a load of unfinished business? Many reasons. Discouragement, fear, distractions. Mood changes, procrastination, laziness. Conflicting responsibilities. Lack of organizational/administrative skill. Failure to follow through.

But one stands higher than all: you assume you'll always have time tomorrow. The lie of procrastination is that it's easier to avoid doing it right now. Those who fulfill their calling understand there will never be a better time than now.

Watch for the red flags. They will undermine your increase. The day will come when, like for Paul, "it's time to stop fighting and rest." But for now we have a few things left to do.

The dangers we face aren't all external or circumstantial. We also have natural points of vulnerability. We'll explore those in the next section.

SEED MONEY

1. Read 2 Timothy 2:1–7 and 2 Timothy 4:1–7. What principles does Paul give Timothy to guide him in completing his mission?

2. "We live in a world that gladly offers to do our thinking for us. It promises to numb us from our pain and entertain us while we stand in line for our own funeral." How has the world tried to do your thinking for you? Think of conventional wisdom, political correctness, or popular-but-wrong ideas.

3. Go back through the list of red flags. Which of them do you most identify with?

4. Make a list of action steps that with God's help will enable you to "push through."

What's Your Handle?
Where Protection Meets Freedom

It all started with that 55-mph speed limit. Americans traded in their muscle cars for Toyotas and slowed down. But a certain segment of the population balked. These people were paid to transport goods to their destinations on time. They believed the new speed limits were hurting their livelihood. So they started working together to cover each other's back. This created a fad. That spawned a counterculture, complete with its own lingo, music, and personal identities.

Everybody, it seemed, rushed out to get a CB radio.

Once the stuff of rescue workers and hobbyists, citizens-band radios became standard equipment. Gone were the official call letters used by the "legal eagles" who actually bought a license. Everybody used a handle—a nickname you gave yourself so people could "grab hold" of you on the radio. They'd say something like, "Break, one-nine. How 'bout that Blue Goose? You got your ears on?"

Assuming that was your handle, you would reply, "Ten-four, good buddy."

No, children, I'm not making this up.

CBs have mostly gone the way of the 55-mph speed limit, though truckers still use them. But you still have a handle—a unique identity by which you can be "grabbed." But not by a Smokey Bear or your good buddy.

The devil is smart but not creative. Have you ever noticed that he usually doesn't nail you with new and interesting temptations? You tend to fall for the same old stuff. Ever wonder why he doesn't try something new?

He doesn't have to. The old one works just fine. He found your handle—the internal weak spots that make any LifeVestor vulnerable to failure.

Thomas à Kempis wrote, "The acknowledgment of our weakness is the first step in repairing our loss." James 1:14 adds, "But each person is tempted when he is lured and enticed by his own desire" (ESV). Over the years we form certain ways of responding to different needs and situations. We do this through thousands of decisions and actions, large and small. This is especially true during those times we try to define life and freedom in our own terms. Those habits become as natural as breathing when you're not depending on the Lord as your strength.

When you drop your guard, out come those invisible handles.

When you think you can handle this one yourself—it's handle time.

When you start leaning on your own understanding, you're an easy target—a sucker for a tempter.

PLUGGING YOUR SPIRITUAL LEAKS

If I was your financial advisor, we'd talk about finding your financial leaks and plugging them up. You can never be free financially free without it. But that's true in other areas as well. If you're going to invest in a future that serves you rather than vice-versa, you must learn to walk in freedom. It's important to identify the places where you tend to go swirling down the proverbial drain. You need to know your handle.

Handles form when we try to fulfill God-given needs in self-pleasing ways. For example, everybody needs love, security, and acceptance—all found in a relationship with Jesus. But what happens when you try to meet those needs all by yourself? More than likely you will fall into one of three behavioral patterns. John refers to them as "lust of the flesh and the lust of the eyes and the boastful pride of life" (1 John 2:16).

Pleasure. Materialism. Pride.

The pursuit of pleasure is an attempt to meet the need for love or to medicate the pain that life often brings. Materialism seeks to find security and safety. Pride seeks to meet a need for acceptance. These handles are as old as Satan's first lie (see Genesis 3:6).

A TRIP TO THE DESERT

> *Jesus, full of the Holy Spirit . . . was led by the Spirit in the wilderness, where for forty days he was tempted by the devil.*
>
> Luke 4:1–2, NRSV

Three things were happening here. Jesus was filled with the Holy Spirit, led by the Spirit, and tempted by the devil. His temptations weren't limited to three satanic curveballs. This was a forty-day season of great displays of power, both temptation and resistance. Jesus emerged victorious.

Much is made of the fact that Jesus resisted His temptations by quoting scripture, and that's valid. But I see a broader picture than that. Underlying all your actions and reactions is a force that's leading you. It can be the Holy Spirit or the patterns of your self-driven life—your "flesh." What you fix your heart and mind on determines who or what is leading you. You must recognize that force and accept responsibility for following it or changing it.

> *Therefore, I urge you, brothers and sisters, in view of God's mercy, to offer your bodies as a living sacrifice, holy and pleasing to God—this is your true and proper worship. Do not conform to the pattern of this world, but be transformed by the renewing of your mind. Then you will be able to test and approve what God's will is—his good, pleasing and perfect will.*
>
> Romans 12:2, NIV

What renews your mind? I've discovered that it matters what I focus on. What I read, watch, study, write about, or meditate on makes a difference. That sets my mind and points my attitude in a certain direction.

My reaction to an event or some wake-up call can also yank me in one direction or another. The Holy Spirit often does this, but the enemy can do it too. Remember this:

> *Temptation isn't only about getting you to commit an act.*
> *It's about changing the force that's leading you.*

The devil's temptations of Jesus weren't just about jumping off temples or eating rocks. They were about disconnecting from the leadership of the Holy Spirit. When someone or something other than the Spirit leads you, the sin is rather automatic. But so is the opposite. "Walk by the Spirit," Paul said, "and you *will not* carry out the desire of the flesh" (Galatians 5:16, emphasis mine).

IDENTIFYING YOUR HANDLE

Part of the victory in all this is in recognizing your own unique handle, your flesh pattern. The devil introduced three types of "Spirit interruptions" to Jesus.

These are consistent with John's three behavioral patterns—pleasure, materialism, and pride. But there are more subtle attempts at interrupting the Spirit's leadership too.

What about the attempt to prove who you are? "If you're *really* the Son of God," the enemy kept repeating. What do you feel compelled to prove? That you're still attractive? That you can buy the same car as your neighbor? That you can handle it (whatever "it" is)?

How about ambition? Maybe the temptation isn't just about material things but about power or a desirable future. How many times have you been led by a fascination with success or control? How many times has the enemy tricked you out of the Spirit's leadership by a reaction that began with, "I'm sick of this"? When Scarlett O'Hara vowed, "As God is my witness I'll never be hungry again," I doubt she was walking in the Spirit.

What about adrenaline? The desire for excitement. A passion for speed, for hurrying things up. Not just get rich, get rich *quick*. Not just action, *impulsive* action. Hurry up. Do it *now*. Forgiveness is easier to get than permission.

Any of these six weapons in the hands of the enemy can change the force that leads you. Jesus recognized what was happening. He continually followed the leading of Holy Spirit. Not just when He was tempted but moment by moment. That's the secret of spiritual protection. Let the Spirit lead you in your daily life decisions and direction. Do that and you stand a better chance of being led by the Spirit in the face of temptation as well. If you're not walking in the Spirit daily, you're defeated before you even start.

SEED MONEY

1. Underlying all your actions and reactions is a force that is leading you. It can be the Holy Spirit or the patterns of your self-driven life—your "flesh." How can you tell when the Holy Spirit is leading you?

2. Read Galatians 5:16–25. Based on this passage, to what degree are you walking in the Spirit vs. walking in the flesh?

3. What are your "handles"? What are your "usual suspects" when it comes to weaknesses or temptations?

4. What would it mean for you to begin walking in the Spirit today? How would you go about positioning your heart and life to make that a reality?

Puppet Strings
Where Protection Meets Eternity

He wrote the song more than forty years ago, but its music and message still haunt me. Sometimes an artist captures the essence of a thing so well, it leaves a lasting impression. Randy Stonehill did it for me when I was a high school senior. In a couple of lines in one song, he described the desperation of the human condition.

Long ago He chose us to inherit all His kingdom
And we were blessed with light
But wandering away we disobeyed Him in the garden
And stumbled into night

And I can feel it in my soul
Now the end is getting near
I can hear the angels weeping
And it's ringing in my ears

We are all like foolish puppets who, desiring to be kings
Now lie pitifully crippled after cutting our own strings.[1]

Jesus had His own description of the world we live in. He also had some clear ideas about how you and I fit into it and how we can be molded by it.

> *"You are the salt of the earth. But what good is salt if it has lost its flavor? Can you make it salty again? It will be thrown out and trampled underfoot as worthless.*
> *"You are the light of the world—like a city on a hilltop that cannot be hidden. No one lights a lamp and then puts it under a basket. Instead, a lamp is placed on a stand, where it gives light to everyone in the house. In the same way, let your good deeds shine out for all to see, so that everyone will praise your heavenly Father."*
> Matthew 5:13–16, NLT

In the preceding verses, Jesus describes the world's reaction to a godly life. It persecutes, reviles, and speaks evil of committed believers (see Matthew 5:912). Now here Jesus describes how Christians relate to the world. You relate to the world as salt relates to the earth and as light relates to the world.

Bottom line: you're either influencing the world or betraying your identity.

THE WORLD OF THE PUPPETS

What's it like to live in a place where the inmates run the asylum? Where people who "now lie pitifully crippled after cutting their own strings" run the show?

It isn't pretty.

Jesus hinted that such a world is a decaying, rotting place that left to its own devices could only poison itself. It needs a preservative; that's what salt was in the first century.

The world is deceptive, however, because it gives off an illusion of life. It can make you feel good enough to think you're living. It can prosper you enough to make you think you have it made. It can stroke your ego enough to convince you that all the praise you receive must be true.

Jesus also called it a dark place. Don't confuse knowledge with light. We live in an age in which knowledge is growing exponentially. Every week brings news of advances in technology. But all this is knowledge without a moral compass. Education without transformation. Knowledge may increase the weapons in our arsenal and the ease with which we use them, but it doesn't make us better people.

THE WORLD'S HOPE FOR SURVIVAL

You're it.

You—believer in Jesus, are the salt.

You are the light in the darkness.

You—the ones Jesus described as poor in spirit.

You—the mourners, the meek, the persecuted for righteousness (see Matthew 5:3–12).

In case you're wondering, there's no plan B. That tells me He thinks pretty highly of what you have to contribute. Even though you may be nothing in the world's eyes, you are priceless in God's. Remember, salt was quite valuable in Jesus' day—much more than the stuff poured out of the blue box today. It was a necessary preservative.

Notice the paradox. The world persecutes and speaks evil of its only hope for survival. That figures.

Salt has other uses, of course. It adds flavor. It makes people thirsty. It purifies. These all speak to the influence you have on your environment. The point is that salt, once it penetrates its environment, changes it. Impacts it. And it does it naturally. You never see a box of Morton's finest, vowing under that umbrella, "I'm gonna season that chicken if it's the last thing I do!" It's salt; it just does it. So do you.

You're also the light of the world. Light is public. It guides and it warns. More to the point, light is something you are, not something you do. You *are* the light of the world because the Father of Light has worked in your life. It's only natural that others will be aware of the light in you.

Jesus said to let your light shine before men. How do you do that? Start by not getting in the way. It's natural for a lamp to illumine. It would take a deliberate act of concealment for light not to shine. So, too, it would take a shame-based act of isolation to hide the work that the Lord is doing.

So much of the Christian life and Christian influence involves a kind of release. You don't have to make God look good or manufacture converts. You just let God be God and let His work speak for itself.

Jesus warns against two extremes. First, He says, take care not to conform to the world's system. We, not the world, are to be the influence on others. Second, take care to avoid a life of isolation. Salt can't preserve anything until you rub it into food. Light isn't light if it's covered up.

Remember, you are the only hope of survival in a desperate, wicked world. And the world will never be changed by your words or human wisdom. It will only be salted by the life of Jesus in you. But the world will also not receive your influence until you get out of your cave and penetrate it.

WHAT ABOUT *YOUR* "FLAVOR"?

Don't overlook the danger here. Christians can lose their "flavor," and you're no exception. Did you know it's possible for salt to lose its flavor? We've learned this the hard way. When salt is overexposed to the elements or has too much contact with the earth, it loses its taste. It still looks the same. It's still sodium chloride. But it's tasteless and useless. Know what people did with it back then? Paved the streets and sidewalks with it. Walked all over it. Just like they'll walk all over you if you become overexposed to the values of the world you're sent to preserve.

The world may persecute you for living a godly life, but they will despise you if you lose your influence. That, not persecution, is the greatest danger you face.

You're a city on a hill, Jesus said. You can't be hidden. It's futile—and offensive—to try to hide the light He has placed in you. That's true even when you're in a crowded public place, surrounded with strangers.

Here's a new definition of insanity: spending one day a week trying to pretend you are something you're not, and six other days trying to hide what you are. Do that and you're no better than a crippled puppet yourself.

Integrity means living in full view with lights shining. Recognizing that, in Oswald Chambers's words, there is "no such thing as a private life or a place to hide in this world."[2] This requires a careful balance. In the world but not of the world. Engage the world and be yourself, under the lordship of Jesus. God will take care of the rest.

Protecting your investment isn't limited to playing defense in your own little world. It also means penetrating a dark world with God's light and life. Here's how one paraphrase puts it:

> Go out into the world uncorrupted, a breath of fresh air in this squalid and polluted society. Provide people with a glimpse of good living and of the living God. Carry the light-giving Message into the night.
>
> Philippians 2:15, MSG

SEED MONEY

1. Read 1 John 1:1–10. What do you think it means to walk in the light? What is the result of a Christian walking in the light?

2. How do you tend to be overexposed to the world? Write about the pressure to conform to the world's standards.

3. "Here's a new definition of insanity: spending one day a week trying to pretend you are something you're not, and six other days trying to hide what you are." How are you tempted to hide your light?

4. What practical ways can you be salt and light during the other six days of week? Be as specific as you can.

FINAL THOUGHT

Back to the ditch. Know why I hit it? Because a ditch was there in the first place. It didn't suddenly appear that lovely summer morning. It had been there all along—I had just ignored it.

I got in the ditch because I was careless. My body was in one place, and my brain was off in another.

I rammed the tree because when I did hit the ditch, I didn't hit the brakes. Seems stupid looking back on it. The ditch was an abrupt first sign of danger. But I didn't interpret it that way. My knee-jerk reaction was, "I can handle this." I handled it, all right.

Care to guess how I finally got out of the ditch and off the tree? Only with help. Somebody with special equipment and tires still on the road had to pull the car to a safe place.

I never drove that car again. Too bad too, because it was very special to me. But I didn't protect my investment, and I paid a price.

If you're living in the wake of your own version of the ditch, I have good news. The ditch, while it can be devastating, doesn't have to be your destiny. You can enlarge your capacity. That's the topic of our next chapter.

CHAPTER 7

Enlarge Your Capacity

The house was quiet. It usually is at 4:30 a.m. I was awake, stretched out facedown on the living room floor.

Fall 1997. I'd been studying the life of Abraham in Genesis. Studying my own life too. Two years earlier I'd been through a "crash and burn" experience. Then a difficult but amazing healing and restoration process. Through it all I had a more intimate relationship with the Lord. My marriage and family relationships were greater than ever. I was serving on the staff of a dynamic church. Just one thing was missing.

"Lord," I asked, "when will I get to be a senior pastor again?"

There as I prayed, Abraham's faith became mine. I received freedom and faith to enter new territory with the Lord.

"You haven't told me what kind of church you want," I heard Him say.

The faith began to rise, and I began to write:

- Hunger for spiritual awakening
- Fight the devil, not each other
- Celebration worship
- Practical, scriptural teaching and preaching
- Balances holiness with grace

- A *healing* place, where broken lives and ministries can be restored
- Balanced between effective evangelism and practical discipleship

These weren't just requests—they were claims. They came with the confidence that God had heard my prayer. There's faith, and then there's *faith*. It was settled as far as I was concerned.

A day later while still studying Abraham's life, I learned a vital lesson. Before God changed Abram's *circumstances*, He changed Abram's *character*. He gave the father of faith a new name and a new identity.

The voice of God again. Quiet. Tender. But dead serious.

> *"I want you to go back to that list you made yesterday.*
> *Start praying I will make you the kind of man who can lead that kind of church."*

Talk about your lessons in praying!

What ensued can only be described as an odyssey. I tend to assume that things are supposed to move in linear fashion. First step A. Then step B. But God doesn't function that way. He's far more concerned with *making me someone* than He is *giving me something*.

I lost count of the number of days that vision collided with disappointment and confusion. Had it been somebody else's life, it would've gotten funny. But it was mine, and I wasn't laughing. After several years of waiting, the vision seemed cold and distant. Disappointments and delays left me with the conclusion that I'd misunderstood God.

Not true. I hadn't misunderstood God—just His priority. I wanted God to enlarge my territory. He was more concerned with enlarging my *capacity*. He has the same interest for you.

God makes fruitful servants even more fruitful. One way He does that is by exposing our hidden "fault lines." And that often comes after great successes. In the next section we explore how our hidden faults are exposed and healed.

Fault Lines
Where Capacity Meets Abundance

How do you feed 5,000 men, plus women and children? That was the assignment. And it wasn't Jesus' job (see Luke 9:10–17).

"Lord, dismiss the crowd so they can go find somewhere to sleep and eat. We're out in the middle of nowhere."

"You feed them," Jesus said.

Get the scene. Jesus had sent the disciples off on a successful mission trip. They had returned with glowing reports of healing, miracles, and changed lives. Jesus wanted to get away, alone with these men so flush with victory.

But a massive crowd caught wind of it and followed Jesus to the desert. The ever-patient teacher stopped to talk with the growing throng about the kingdom of God. And between the Master and the masses were these miracle workers.

"You feed them."

With that mission the disciples had two choices: calculate or connect. Figure it or faith it. Come on, guys! You just sent demons fleeing. This was something akin to an Advanced Miracle Working class. But they missed the connection and calculated (see John 6:6–7). They saw no connection between their previous miracles and the need they now faced.

I'm no different. I often think I've scored one for the home team and should get to relax. Celebrate. Sign a few autographs. Maybe get endorsement deals from Bible dealers. But the Lord has different ideas. He raises the bar and asks me to take it to the next level.

"You feed them."

Suddenly I'm confronted with the reality that, like the twelve, I don't have it all together yet. Instead of displaying my awesomeness, I'm revealing my fault lines.

TRACING THE CRACKS

I don't know geology, but I know generally what they mean when scientists use the word *fault*. Deep in the foundations of the earth are cracks that produce shifts in the earth's foundation. We experience them as earthquakes. Destructive and deadly, they leave scars on lives and landscapes that time alone doesn't fix. All the result of faults that seemed nonexistent a day earlier.

Faults show up in the Bible too.

> *Admit your faults to one another and pray for each other so that you may be healed. The earnest prayer of a righteous man has great power and wonderful results.*
>
> James 5:16, TLB

Even "righteous men" have faults. And who better to pray for our faults than someone who is painfully aware of their own?

Of course, we have other names for faults. You can call them flaws or weaknesses, besetting sins or vices. But *fault,* understood in the context of a geologist, provides a beautiful word picture. Like California's San Andreas Fault, we all have cracks in our foundation. They have different causes, such as unhealed hurts, unfulfilled desires, or self-will. But regardless of how they got there, we have them.

Ever notice how earthquakes tend to show up at the same places again and again? It's because of the underlying fault lines. We do that too. We "quake" just above our own fault lines. Rarely is it something new—just the latest manifestation of the same old cracks in our foundation.

Some faults are obvious to us; others we're blind to. Suppose I asked Carrie, my daughter, "What are your faults?" Assuming she was honest, she would give me her perspective on her weaknesses. But as her father, I have a perspective she isn't aware of. I may see things that to her, in this stage of her life, are miniscule, while to me they look massive. That's why the psalmist prayed,

> *Who perceives his unintentional sins?*
> *Cleanse me from my hidden faults.*
>
> Psalm 19:12, HCSB

We're all particularly sensitive to faults in others that mirror our own. When I see laziness in others it hits a nerve; that's one of the faults I am aware of in myself. Same goes for sloppiness or hotheadedness. That's why we should be careful about pointing out the cracks we see in others. Jesus said to take care of the beam in your own eye before picking the speck out of your brother's (see Luke 6:41–42).

THREE RESPONSES

I've observed three responses in people who are confronted with their faults. Some people *hide*. Remember Adam and Eve in the Garden of Eden? They tried to hide from the presence of the Lord. Lotta good that did!

Shame tells us that if others know our faults they'll reject us. So we cover them, bury them. The sad joke is, by hiding our fundamental flaws we create even more faults. What's more, our attempts to conceal only set us (and others) up for the quake to come. Hidden faults never stay hidden forever.

Other people respond to their faults by *hurling*. Here's an old favorite from childhood: "It's not my fault!" We try to justify our own bad behavior by shifting the focus or hurling the blame.

Adam did it: "The woman . . ."

Eve did too: "The serpent . . ."

We've been hurling ever since.

Hurling takes on many forms beyond direct blaming. Sometimes we hurl in our heads. We never actually say it's someone else's fault. We just think it. Or act like it. Or carry out some stunt to punish them for inconveniences caused by our own fault lines.

God offers a more productive alternative. It's called *healing*. To our "That's just who I am" excuses, Jesus replies, "I died to *change* who you are." He offers us a pathway of courageous faith that leads to changed life.

Unlike geological plates and pressure points, character faults can be mended. That starts with believing they can. But right behind that comes the humbling truth we must face:

We can't heal our own faults. And hidden faults just get faultier.

The pathway to healing is through courageous honesty. With ourselves. With God. With other believers. Every healthy believer is honest with somebody about his or her own fault lines. And every healthy believer is a safe place for others to share the same.

You need somebody you trust to listen sympathetically and pray for you. As you open up to safe people about your fault lines, you make yourself teachable. Accountable. Approachable. Healable!

> *The urgent request of a righteous person is very powerful in its effect.*
> James 5:16, HCSB

Do you believe that? So what makes a person "righteous"? The fact that they're actively pursuing their own growth, healing, and holiness. And they, too, have confessed their faults to someone else.

Nobody likes it when their fault lines are exposed. Nor do they like living in the aftershock of somebody else's quake. But faults are healable when we get teachable. And humble. Does that take courage? Yep. But it's the only way to move forward in the development of character.

Growth points often come disguised as harsh adversity. The good news is that you have a living leadership legacy that has faced many of the same stretch points as you. We explore that spiritual support community in the next section.

SEED MONEY

1. Read James 5:13–18. What promises are made to those who are transparent with others in the body of Christ?

2. What are some of the areas of our lives that James says we are to keep exposed to other believers? How easy is it for you to do that?

3. Take a spiritual inventory of your previous life experiences, good or bad. What significant experiences has the Lord carried you through in the past? What have you learned from those experiences?

4. "You need somebody you trust to listen sympathetically and pray for you." Who is that for you? How often do you share your needs and challenges with someone you trust? How easy or difficult is that for you? Who can you reach out to this week to spend time with?

Friends in High Places
Where Capacity Meets Leadership

Join me at the starting line. You're about to take off on this marathon. Your coach is the Lord Jesus, the Author of your faith. Under His direction you've cast aside any hindering weights. You clear your way of any sin that might entangle you. At His signal, you're off! And following His wise counsel, you've focused your attention on Him.

You lengthen your stride and settle in. You know this is no sprint; you're in it for the long run and this won't be easy. But about the time you reach your first obstacle, God has a surprise for you. You are not alone! You're surrounded by a great cloud of witnesses! They're "in the grandstands" cheering you on.

These aren't just any witnesses. They're your "friends in high places"—your legacy of leadership. These people have run the same race and faced the same obstacles you face. The Bible presents this gallery of greatness as models of faith and perseverance. These are the ones who . . .

> *By faith conquered kingdoms, performed acts of righteousness, obtained promises, shut the mouths of lions, quenched the power of fire, escaped the edge of the sword, from weakness were made strong, became mighty in war, put foreign armies to flight. Women received back their dead by resurrection; and others were tortured, not accepting their release, so that they might obtain a better resurrection; and others experienced mockings and scourgings, yes, also chains and imprisonment.*
>
> Hebrews 11:33–37

These aren't just dead figures from the past. Their faith—and witness—live on. They're watching you. Rooting for you. Believing in you. Teaching you. They're here to testify that you, too, can make it. They also testify of the tools our Father uses to deepen your message and enlarge that influence.

OVERWHELMING ODDS

As you run, you'll face incredible odds against finishing. Your back will be to the wall. But in the grandstands is Gideon, and he's here to testify. He faced a marauding army of Midianites with only three hundred men. Armed only with jugs and torches, he was fired by the faithfulness of God (see Judges 6–8). He'll tell you that God put him there on purpose. He'll also declare, "You can be victorious, even when the odds are against you. I subdued kingdoms, and so can you!"

RAW DEALS

You've probably figured out by now, life isn't fair. Sometimes people give you a raw deal, even when you've done everything you know to live with honor and integrity. The temptation is to "sink to their level." But there's Joseph with a different story. He was rejected, trafficked, sexually harassed, falsely accused, jailed, and forgotten. Is he bitter? No. He's cheering you on: "You can work righteousness, even when it seems impossible. What they meant for evil, God meant for good" (see Genesis 37–50).

SIDE STREETS

You'll face times when it seems futile to trust God's promises because He seems to be taking you on a detour. Why does everybody else get to experience the blessings that are supposed to be yours? But in the crowd you can hear the voice of Abraham (see Genesis 12–23). There's a man who understood detours. Ridiculously long delays. But he's calling your name, saying, "You can trust God. I waited for years, and He didn't fail me. I received His promises."

CHEAP SHOTS

As you strive for excellence, you'll face cheap shots from jealous people in the mediocre majority. They'll even lie or falsely accuse you. But in the stands is

Daniel, a model of an excellent spirit (see Daniel 6:3). He's cheering you on, saying, "You can experience an extraordinary life! I stopped the mouths of lions, and so can you. You can't stop the cheap shots from coming, but by God's grace you can maintain a spirit of excellence."

JERK BOSSES

You will go through times of intense pressure. Sometimes that pressure comes from egotistical, abusive people in authority. The temptation will be to compromise or to seek an escape or a way to get even. But in the crowd are Shadrach, Meshach, and Abednego. They're testifying to the presence of God in the middle of the fire (see Daniel 3:1–30), cheering you on, saying, "Don't compromise. Face that inferno! With Jesus with you, you can quench the violence of the fire!"

ANGRY NEIGHBORS

You will encounter people who, with or without cause, hate the fact that you exist. Your temptation will be to fear them because of their hostility. You'll feel outnumbered and afraid. But in the stands is Elisha, cheering you on, saying, "You can find security in the crisis. I escaped the edge of the sword, and so can you (see 2 Kings 6:8–23). Greater is He who is you than he who is in the world" (1 John 4:4).

STUPID CHOICES

Chances are, you'll make choices you regret. You're going to get weak at times. Sometimes you will stumble and fall and get up bloody and wounded. What's more, God will allow you to live with the consequences of those choices. You'll be tempted to assume there's no future for failures. But in the stands is Samson, who knew what it meant to be a colossal failure. He had the blindness and scars to show for it (see Judges 16:1–31). He testifies of the grace of our God, that in your weakness you can be made strong.

TAUNTING GIANTS

It's one thing when somebody challenges you. It's another when they challenge and mock the name of the Christ you serve. Now you're faced with defending

God's name against someone bigger, smarter, and meaner than you. But listen closely to the cheering crowd. You will hear David saying, "You can conquer the giants, and become valiant in battle" (see 1 Samuel 17).

BAFFLING SITUATIONS

You will face situations that are so confusing, so baffling, you're at a loss what to do. But in the stands is Jehoshaphat. He knows sometimes God leads us into impossible situations so He can show the world His glory. When faced with a Moabite invasion, Jehoshaphat led his people to call on the Lord. His testimony to you is, "Your problems are God's opportunities. He took our impossible problem and sent foreign armies running the other way" (see 2 Chronicles 20:1–25).

BROKEN HEARTS

Sooner or later, your heart will be shattered by pain that God could have prevented but didn't. You may be angry with God or have a hard time understanding why He would allow something like this to happen. But listen closely to the grandstands and perhaps you will hear Elijah. He's shouting, "You can be a man or woman of God, not in spite of your broken heart, but *because* of it" (see 1 Kings 17:17–23).

Well, there they are. Ten methods God uses to enlarge your legacy. My guess is, if you've followed Him for any length of time, you already know what I'm talking about.

Despite the uncertainty, hurt, or fierce attacks, somebody's watching out for you. Cheering you on. Isn't that good to know? However, certain investments in your growth only you can provide. We explore that in the next section.

SEED MONEY

1. Which of these ten tools God uses is most real to you now? Who in the Bible or history or your life is an example to you that you aren't alone in your struggles?

2. Read Psalm 91. How does it tell you to respond to the challenges of your faith? What promises does God make to His people when they face great opposition?

3. "Your problems are God's opportunities." Reframe a current problem you have and reflect how it may be an opportunity to experience God's work in your life. Where's God in all this? How does Psalm 91 speak to your situation?

4. If the problem you are dealing with is actually an opportunity, how will you act differently? What actions would you take to walk in the solution rather than walking in the problem?

Investing in the Investor
Where Capacity Meets Increase

His innovative ministry shook and shaped the town where he lived. He started a church from scratch and tossed tradition on its ear. He insisted that worship services be events people would actually enjoy attending. His preaching was simple and plain. He laced his sermons with word pictures, practical application, and charisma.

He led his people to share God's love with a system of literature distribution and visitation. In a matter of months his church went from mission to mega.

More than a thousand people were attending his Thursday night Bible study.

He was a prayer warrior. This guy spent an hour a day praying only for the Jews! Another hour daily in general prayer and meditation. An hour and a half in breakfast and family prayers. Six hours in prayer and devotional reading on Sundays.

Then there was the revival. Returning from the Middle East, he found his town spiritually awakened by a fresh move of the Spirit. People came nightly to hear him preach the gospel. Hundreds came to Christ. Without question, he was one of the greatest Christian leaders of any generation.

He died in 1843.

Age—29.

Name—Robert Murray McCheyne. As he lay on his deathbed, he said to the friend beside him,

> *"God gave me a horse to ride and message to deliver.*
> *Alas, I have killed the horse, and now I cannot deliver the message!"*

No use playing "what if" in his case. Asking you the tough questions about *your* life is another story. And since I'm typing this half-sick, mentally tired, eating everything in sight, I'll join the party.

"Physician, heal thyself," Jesus said, quoting the popular proverb (Luke 4:23, KJV). Another way of saying: Plumber, fix your own leaks. Teacher, go back to school.

LifeVestor, invest in yourself. A significant part of expecting a future return is seeing to it you'll actually be around to enjoy it.

Not all investments in your future involve mashing the gas pedal. To enlarge your capacity, at times you'll have to slow down or stop. You'll need to go into maintenance mode and take care of yourself. In this section we'll explore that. How can you increase your results by increasing your strength and health?

Years ago a Detroit homeowner went to check on his five-bedroom house. Wasn't there. I don't mean the tenants had moved out. I mean, the *house* had skipped town. Completely baffled, he asked the *Detroit Free Press* to help him investigate. A reporter learned the house had been torn down and the deed to the empty lot was *now* in someone else's name. Several years had passed since the homeowner left town. He left no forwarding address and failed to arrange for someone to keep the property in repair. The city declared the house an eyesore and ordered it torn down. All because of negligence.

Bad enough when it's a building. *Devastating* when it's your body, your brain, or your spirit.

You want to see an increase? It's going to take some SelfVesting. Encouraging the encourager. Giving to the giver. Caring for the caregiver. This is what keeps you from being a codependent workaholic. This is what keeps you from gambling with your future. This is what keeps you from being . . . well, *dead!*

IT ALL STARTS WITH STOPPING

My sister and I used to make mud tea. We didn't call it that, nor did we drink the swill. But when we were small we'd play around outside with spare dishes. One of our concoctions involved mixing a little dirt 'n' water to make a pretend drink. When we stirred our little elixir, the water would take on that irresistible shade of brown. When we stopped stirring, it stayed muddy. But when we gave it a rest and went off to other pursuits, the water was always clearer when we returned. The mud had settled to the bottom.

Your life is like that glass in our backyard. Stir it up, it gets muddy. It's easy to become confused, distorted, foggy, and dull. Under the pressure of circumstances, it's harder to see issues clearly. Even harder to make good decisions.

Had any "muddy water days" lately? The smart phone won't quit buzzing. The baby won't stop crying. Everybody needs your help at the same time. You have major, life-changing decisions to make. You have a week's worth of money to pay a month's worth of bills. You spend the entire day running about thirty minutes behind. Then you turn on the radio and some clown's singing, "It's a Beautiful Morning."

You aren't alone. The Bible is full of examples of people whose lives were "stirred up." In Psalm 46 a psalmist writes to frustrated, anxious, and confused people who felt as though the earth was being removed and the mountains were being shoved into the sea. His answer?

> "Be still [stop striving]
> and know that I am God."
>
> Psalm 46:10, NIV & NASB

David told the Lord on one occasion that he was restless. "Please listen and answer me, for I am overwhelmed by my troubles," he said (Psalm 55:2, NLT). But the lesson he learned from that experience was priceless:

> Pile your troubles on GOD's shoulders—he'll carry your load, he'll
> help you out.
> He'll never let good people topple into ruin.
>
> Psalm 55:22, MSG

Isaiah understood that experience. "Even youths grow tired and weary, and young men stumble and fall" (Isaiah 40:30, NIV). Why do youths grow tired and weary? Why do young men, in the prime of their strength, stumble and fall? Because they haven't learned to renew their strength (see Isaiah 40:31). And they haven't recognized the priceless value of resting in the Lord.

Have you ever noticed that God's strategy is different from ours? First, you wait, then you work. First, you rest, then you take off. When God created a world with twenty-four time zones, the evening came first. Sleep comes first. Work comes later. That's far removed from our typical mindset, expressed by actress Bette Davis:

"I am doomed to an eternity of compulsive work. No set goal achieved satisfies. Success only breeds a new goal. The golden apple devoured has seeds. It is endless."

We work and go until we wear ourselves out, then rest, usually not by choice.

In God's way of doing things, you work in the stance of "restedness." Quiet, then action.

Remember Joshua and Jericho? When the Israelites reached Canaan, did they charge straight into the Jordan? No. Joshua sounded the red alert, then they took three days to think about it, rest on it, and get ready. Rest first, then came the battle.

Think about the book of Acts. There you find an incredible account of the explosive growth of the early church. Action everywhere—traveling, witnessing, establishing churches. But before all the action—stillness. Preceding Pentecost you see an entire chapter of quiet, rest, prayer, and waiting on God.

Plan on it. When life gets crazy and you need time to be refreshed, something nearly always comes up. Life has declared war on anything that renews your strength. If the devil can't keep you off the narrow road, he'll cut your brake lines.

"Martha, dear Martha [substitute your name here], you're fussing far too much and getting yourself worked up over nothing. One thing only is essential, and Mary has chosen it—it's the main course, and won't be taken from her."

Luke 10:41–42, MSG

When you're frenzied and frustrated, and it makes no sense to stop, you have to say no. And to the most difficult person of all—yourself. The size of the vision, the possibilities, the potential impact of the increase all cry out . . .

Don't just do something. Stand there.

Or as you will see in the next section, sometimes to make us stronger, the message is even louder:

Don't stop doing what you're doing. Hang in there.

SEED MONEY

1. Read Luke 10:38–42. What would it look like to carve out some "Mary" time in your schedule?

2. "Life has declared war on anything that renews your strength." What examples do you see of this in your own life? Be as specific as possible.

3. LifeVestor, invest in yourself. How do you need to do that? In what areas—physical, spiritual, mental, emotional, relational?

4. Name at least one thing you will do this week for the express purpose of rest or renewing your strength.

The Guaranteed Way to Profit
Where Capacity Meets Freedom

"This is warfare," Robin said.

"It's God!" I snapped back, dispirited and resigned. "Let's just go home."

There. Now you know what we fight about at my house.

THE DAY FROM HELL

It was the day from hell that started with a hard funeral. I was the speaker. Some funerals virtually preach themselves; this one didn't. My message to the grieving family and friends was the same verse I mentioned previously:

> *"Be still—stop striving—*
> *and know that He is God.*
>
> Psalm 46:10

Boy, did that message flip over on my head.

It was Monday. We'd survived a harried and stressful Sunday, during a harried and stressful summer. But this was the Monday when the scenery was to change. With the help of my wonderful office staff, we had scheduled a trip to the mountains to write.

Actually, to write this book.

A little proverbial advice, for what it's worth: beware of trying to change your scenery on Monday.

Anyway, it would be a working trip, surrounded by mountain grandeur. We would enjoy a respite from the usual busy schedule. I would have a feeling of accomplishment on the other side. But first I had to prepare to say something to a grieving family needing help and hope. I also had to attend to a few other necessary distractions. It felt like I was trying to push a huge emotional rock up a mountain. But I also had to stop and give interviews and make a hundred little decisions along the way.

Somewhere after the fact, I heard the Lord say, "Why didn't you ask Me for help?"

We finally hit the road about 1:30, still trying to unwind from two stressful days. We'd been gone about forty-five minutes when I was nailed by a small-town speed trap. Carelessly, on a five-lane road leaving town, I screeched through Mayberry at a blistering 50 mph in a 35-mph zone. The only other vehicle in sight was a West Texas version of Barney Fife. Not that I'm bitter or anything.

To make up for lost time I did some laptop work in the car and let Robin drive. I wrote until my battery ran out. Not far from our destination, I resumed the command of the *Enterprise*.

And got *another* ticket.

"I quit! I quit! I'm obviously doing 70 in a 55 world! And evidently, I'm the worst driver in the history of driving. A complete failure as a human being." There was more to my journal rant that evening, but you get the point.

We (very slowly) reached the hotel, and once in the room, I plugged in my computer cord to recharge the battery. The cord somehow failed. I called, and the manufacturer said they couldn't get me a new one until Wednesday morning. I'd come here to write, and I was dead in the water.

Past the journal rant, I heard the Lord saying,

"I'm just trying to get you to slow down. The tickets were just a metaphor for a larger issue. You can't write if you can't listen. And right now, you're not listening. And since when do you have to have a computer to meet Me, to hear from Me?"

I began to regain what little sense and sensitivity I had left. I realized God's plan was different from my mission. His idea was rest, then work. Truth is, I was trying to write from an exhausted heart. I needed some "be still" time. I needed to hear my own sermon to the grieving family. I told the Lord I was tired of pushing that rock up the hill. He could either push it or let it run over me.

The next day I was on the patio of our hotel room. Admiring the stunning scenery—and suffering the indignity of having to use a pen and a legal pad—I read this in my Bible:

A man of great anger will bear the penalty,
For if you rescue him, you will only have to do it again.
Listen to counsel and accept discipline,
That you may be wise the rest of your days.

Proverbs 19:19–20

Yep, I was right. It was God. I needed a meltdown so I could actually "listen to counsel and accept discipline." A "man of great anger" (I'm *sure* that can't mean me!) refuses to do that. When discipline comes, my responsibility is clear. I have to reel in the anger and accept the direction the Lord is taking me.

In that context, the discipline of the Lord was to slow down (literally) and unplug (literally). By having to handwrite a book outline and force my spirit to be still, I moved from frustration to anger to depression to surrender . . . back to quietness again. And *there* I began to hear the Lord speak.

GOD'S STRANGE PLAN TO PROFIT YOU

God wants to enlarge your capacity. He also wants you to experience freedom. By enduring sometimes-hard seasons today, we create seasons of blessing in the future. Like an athletic champion, this requires seasons of enforced learning. Is that pleasant? Hardly. But it's worth it.

Discipline can be brutal sometimes. It can feel endless. But it serves a purpose in God's plan that little else can. According to the writer of Hebrews, it's God's foolproof plan to profit His children.

> *In your struggle against sin you have not yet resisted to the point of shedding your blood. And have you forgotten the exhortation that addresses you as sons?*
>
> *"My son, do not regard lightly the discipline of the Lord,*
> *nor be weary when reproved by him.*
> *For the Lord disciplines the one he loves,*
> *and chastises every son whom he receives."*
>
> Hebrews 12:4–6, ESV

The word translated "discipline" means "enforced learning" in Greek. It's the learning that takes place when we run out of other options, when all we have left is God's truth and His desires. But despite what our human nature might think, God isn't being stubborn or harsh. Discipline expresses His love. It reveals

His desire to transform us from spiritual children to mature adults. Discipline declares, "You have a Father, and you have a future!"

God's discipline lets us know how far we have to go. Sometimes we claim progress as perfection; God has other ideas. So He encourages us not to take His discipline lightly. Taking it lightly today means taking it again tomorrow. Learning from it today can mean being released from it tomorrow.

Make no mistake, discipline is a form of correction. It's a call for change. That's the difference between discipline and spiritual warfare. If what you're encountering is a form of discipline, the message will be clear: change this. On the day of my mountain misery, there was no doubting the message.

The Lord disciplines us in person, not through some chain of command. That's both frightening and comforting. He who can destroy you with a thought comes to you as a Father to build you up. God loves you enough not to leave you to flounder where you are. He insists that you move forward.

Discipline often shows up as hardship. In case you had any doubts, this hurts. Your adversity can be a form of God's discipline that requires your patient endurance. You may be doing something wrong. Or maybe you're untrained or unfaithful in doing something right. In either case, hardness is a good thing; it's serving a higher purpose.

Discipline is proof of sonship (see Hebrews 12:7). God doesn't discipline unbelievers. His name and credibility aren't attached to them. They have no covenant with Him. We do. Discipline is our connecting point to God's holiness. God's discipline will take us where self-discipline can't and won't.

Good news! Discipline *always* has an "afterward"—a harvest of righteousness and peace. Often you see that in your lifetime. Sometimes the reward waits for you in heaven.

So where are you facing hardship? What are the life lessons God is teaching? What corrections is He making? What comfort zones is He bumping or yanking you out of? Don't take it lightly. He's *profiting* you.

SEED MONEY

1. Read Hebrews 12:3–17. Describe in your own words the profit that comes from discipline. How did Esau miss it? How can you?

2. What "rude interruptions" or in-your-face interventions have you received from God lately? Does it make a difference to you what the source is?

3. "God's discipline lets us know how far we have to go. Sometimes we claim progress as perfection; God has other ideas." What has God's discipline taught you lately about how far you have to go?

4. Based on the lessons learned from God's discipline, what is one thing you can do differently to align your life more to God's purposes?

Tastes of Heaven
Where Capacity Meets Eternity

It was a day of surprises. If you had told me the Friday before what I would experience that Saturday, I wouldn't have believed you. I don't know whether I would have stayed in bed all day or sat up sleepless the night before. That Saturday years ago was a taste of heaven.

When the Lord enlarges your capacity, He doesn't limit it to what you can do in the moment. He also increases the scope of your victory and the reach of your influence. That includes your lifetime and earthly influence after you're gone, as well as your eternal impact. You may forget or never know the impact of your life. But God does.

THE RACE

Pinewood Derby races are a big event. Boys and dads work together to transform a block of wood into a race car. They cut it to shape, paint it, and add wheels, decals, and other sporty stuff. Then they put them to the test on a track. Think small-scale indoor drag racing.

Anyone who knows me knows I'm no engineer or craftsman. Put my son, then age eight, together with me on such a project, it was like the blind leading the blind. So it was par for the course that Joel sacked out at 9:00 the Friday night before the race. And when I finally went to bed, the car was still wet with paint and had no wheels.

How do you prepare your son to lose when he's dreaming of glory? How do you brace him for the fact that there are more than thirty other boys with cars? And many of them have been doing this for several years. How do you explain that the fun was in the working together, even if we didn't win a single race?

I did the best I could. I had him talked into being satisfied if he won a race or two. So that Saturday morning we somehow got our wheels attached and took our still-sticky car to test it out and see how we'd done.

He won the whole thing.

Beat 'em all.

Mamma giggled all the way home. I was in shock. The boy was beaming. He took the trophy. Hey, Peter on the water, the Mets in '69, Namath in the Super Bowl—those were upsets. We're talkin' miracle here!

Who'd a thought it? Certainly not me. I had spent so much time bracing him to lose, the thought had never occurred to us that he might actually win. But win he did. And teach—the Lord did.

We Christians love to talk and sing about heaven. We love to describe it in terms so familiar you'd think we had already been there for years. But the truth is, the Lord still has breathtaking surprises waiting for us there. I believe in heaven we're going to be surprised that we are standing in a place of victory. We've grown so accustomed to being, feeling, and acting whipped, victory may be a strange thing.

THE CONCERT

But the lessons weren't over. That night we went to a concert. Great concert, good fellowship, outstanding worship. It was a reunion of sorts too. I ran into some people there I hadn't seen in years. But once in their lives, when they were children, I had been their pastor. Many of them had to remind me of their names. Many of them reminded me of precious other things.

"You baptized me."

"You led me to Christ."

"I've missed you!"

Know what's stranger than winning when you expected to lose? It's finding out you're *somebody* when you thought you were just another *nobody*.

Amid the joy of reunion, it was hard to know how to feel. I was reminded again how easy it is to dismiss our influence on others. Fact is, for many people it's life-changing. But some of the ways we've touched other people's lives will remain hidden until we see Jesus—and see them.

THE RETREAT

I had a similar experience at a youth retreat where I led with a group of people I'd not seen for almost a decade. It was surprising. I was surprised at the warmth of their response, at the depth of their respect for me, at how many names I remembered. And surprised how natural it still felt to love them, even though I hadn't seen them in so long a time.

You can imagine the rush of memories. Funny ones. Sad ones. Powerful ones. Mostly I remembered the people whose lives I had touched, and whose lives had touched mine. In the faces of teenagers who were three-to-five years old when I last saw them, I saw the images of their older brothers and sisters, most of whom had married at least once by then. Nearly all had children. Greg was in Atlanta, Gerald somewhere in Florida, Lisa in Texas. Many had scattered throughout Mississippi. Mike was in the ministry, Mason ran a farm, Buddy went to prison, Scotty committed suicide. Some of them were deacons, some were devils. Either way, they were still surprisingly important to me.

I had only lived around these people for a year. I'd written off my ministry there as a growth time for me. We saw a few good things happen, but I figured it was otherwise forgettable for them.

Boy, was I wrong about them.

Boy, was I wrong about me.

THE KINGDOM

Never underestimate the power of your influence. And don't let it surprise you that God can use little ol' you. Jesus gave a couple of illustrations of the kingdom of God that make the point. In both, something small and seemingly insignificant becomes something huge, with permeating influence.

"What is the Kingdom of God like? What shall I compare it with? It is like this. A man takes a mustard seed and plants it in his field. The plant grows and becomes a tree, and the birds make their nests in its branches." Again Jesus asked, "What shall I compare the Kingdom of God with? It is like this. A woman takes some yeast and mixes it with a bushel of flour until the whole batch of dough rises."

Luke 13:18–21, GNT

Apart to itself the kingdom has no influence. Only as the seed falls into the ground or the yeast penetrates the flour is its influence felt. So also the kingdom of God flourishes when it penetrates the kingdom of this world. Can you be a kingdom influence? Yes, but you must be willing to be "planted" in someone else's life to make it happen.

The kingdom does its best work in the secret places. Buried in the soil, the mustard seed grows. Immersed in the dough, the yeast permeates the bread. Quietly working in the lives of people that Jesus loves, God's kingdom grows. Can you be an influence? Sure, so long as you don't have to be famous to be useful.

The growth of the kingdom is a normal, expected event. It's natural for a seed to grow and for leavened bread to rise. It is just as natural for the kingdom of God to grow. We don't have to manufacture it. We just have to be faithful participants and let God do the work. Can you be an influence? Yes, so long as you don't confuse your job with His.

The kingdom transforms natural enemies into friends. Interesting. The mustard, which would be eaten by the birds in seed form, becomes a haven for the birds as it grows and flourishes. This is a picture of love and forgiveness. As the kingdom grows, it reaches out in love to those who persecute, hate, and seek to destroy it. Can you be an influence? Yes, to the degree that you are willing to express His love to anybody.

And there in the reunion and teaching about the kingdom is another surprise. In heaven we'll spend eternity hearing the testimonies of people whose lives we touched. Only we never knew it. The life investments you make in people and in eternity *will* revisit you, my friend. You may have forgotten or dismissed it. But your Father has other ideas.

SEED MONEY

1. Read Acts 4:31–35 and notice the action words. What do these verses suggest about the key to the church's influence?

2. "Never underestimate the power of your influence." Who are the primary people in your realm of influence today? What kind of influence do you have on them? What does that suggest about your choices and priorities?

3. Do you find it hard to love certain people because of outward characteristics? Or bad past experiences? How can the Holy Spirit enable you to love people who are hard to love?

4. Of the actions mentioned in Acts 4:31–35, what specific action will you focus on this week to increase your spiritual capacity?

FINAL THOUGHT

Remember that vision for a new ministry I told you about? A friend suggested something different. "Pray about starting a new work," he said.

I did. And I did. And that church is thriving under different leadership today.

For seven years there I had some of the most fulfilling times of my life. Until once again I reached the limits of my capacity and character. That's a story for another day. But looking back on it, the message is as clear today as it was back then. God is more concerned with enlarging my capacity than enlarging my territory. The same is true for you.

During that dreaming stage, I once wrote in my journal, "I am so tired of hearing that my solution is to wait." Too bad. I still had to give God time to finish what He started. And that's the topic of our next chapter.

CHAPTER 8

Give It Time

A rewrite of an old story . . .

Will Martin was a vocational evangelist whose wife died, leaving him with two sons, ages eight and ten. Hard as it was, he sought to be a faithful dad and faithful evangelist. He rearranged his schedule to limit the number of days he was away. And he made himself a promise: whenever he went away overnight, he would bring his sons a special gift.

Then came the day Will was wheels-up on the plane and realized he'd forgotten to pick up something for his boys. So he conceived a plan.

The boys were ready to see their dad and excited to get inside his suitcase.

"Don't even bother, guys," Dad said. "There's nothing in there. Tomorrow morning, as soon as Target opens, I'm taking you there to buy anything you want."

"Dad, you don't *mean* it!"

"I mean it."

It was Christmas in August. And true to his word, Will and his sons were there when the doors opened.

First stop—the candy and nuts counter with its collection of hot nuts, popcorn, and snacks. The boys had already landed on what they wanted.

"Dad, can we have some candy?"

"I told you," Will replied, "you can have anything you want. But before you decide that, let's look some more."

The next stop was clothes and shoes. The boys found some things they really liked.

"*Dad*," they said, "you think we could get whole new outfits?"

"Sure, if that's what you want. But let's keep looking."

Around to the sporting goods section, where the boys started playing with new basketballs.

"Oh *Dad*," one exclaimed, "could we *possibly* get a new basketball?"

"I told you, you can have anything you want. But let's check one more place before you decide."

In the electronics department in the back of the store, they stopped in front of the video games cabinet. There the boys got lost in their favorite Xbox titles. Both turned to peer into their dad's eyes. Did he really mean what he'd promised?

"Oh *Daddy!* Do you think we could each get a video game?"

"Boys, I told you," Will said. "You can have anything you want. And I keep my promises."

Then it dawned on one of them.

"Oh. But we don't have a console. We can't play the games if we don't have the Xbox."

"Well, let's go talk to that man behind the counter," Will suggested.

"Hi, I'm Will Martin—" Will started.

"Oh yes, Mr. Martin. We have your console right here."

Never have two sets of eyes opened so widely. And they walked out of the store with two games and a new Xbox One X.

Will intended to buy that the entire time. He even called to ask them to hold a game console for him, just in case. But he took his boys on a scenic route to their ultimate destination.

Bet they were glad they didn't stop at the candy counter.

You may be on a scenic route of your own. Maybe you anticipated that. Often we don't. I don't know about you, but I like my directions and answers in straight, short lines. If I'm at point A, I want the nearest and fastest line to point B. Funny how God has His own plans about how to get me there.

Someone once said, "Waiting on the Lord is like sitting on a concrete bench." It's easy enough at first, but over time can get harder and harder. Nevertheless God reserves His greatest blessings for those who trust Him to finish what He started. That involves time, process, and progress . . . and yes, waiting.

The scenic route and the discipline of waiting—at this seventh stage in the LifeVesting cycle, at some point the only thing missing is time. But as you will see, waiting is anything but passive. And there's more than one way to wait. Waiting is one of God's tools to test our faith and strengthen our resolve. And believe it or not, learning to wait can be an extraordinary source of joy and delight.

God, the Goose, and the Golden Egg
Where Waiting Meets Abundance

Remember Aesop's fable about the goose and the golden egg? The implications and applications are powerful.

The fable describes a poor farmer who one day found a glittering golden egg in the nest of his pet goose. At first he thought it was a practical joke. But he had it appraised—the egg was pure gold!

The farmer couldn't believe his good fortune. And it happened again the next day, and the next. Day after day, he awakened, rushed to the nest, and found another golden egg. He became fabulously wealthy; it all seemed too good to be true.

But as his wealth grew, so did his greed and impatience. Unwilling to settle for one daily egg, the farmer decided to kill the goose and collect them all at once. But the goose was empty. No golden eggs, and now no way to get any more. The farmer had destroyed the goose that produced them.

While this story isn't in the Bible, it reflects many biblical principles. And it cuts to the heart of LifeVesting.

IDENTIFYING YOUR "GOOSE"

When God wants to give us "golden eggs," He usually sends us a "goose" to produce them. Your golden egg can be anything of value. And God can certainly speak value into existence.

Money? Easy.

Strength? Yep.

Wisdom? Absolutely.

Fulfilled dream? Sure.

But the Lord usually doesn't magically shovel those things directly to us. Instead, He gives us brains, bodies, abilities, and helpful people. Your geese are sources God uses to produce value you want. But unlike the fable, you have more than one goose. You have a gaggle of them.

CARING FOR THE GOOSE

Want to ensure an abundant supply of good things (golden eggs)? Take care of God's channels for receiving them (the geese). This includes your body, your relationships, your finances, and your abilities.

This reflects the biblical principle of stewardship (1 Corinthians 6:19–20). Nothing you have belongs to you. It's all a God-given trust for you to manage.

Caring for your goose means *feeding* it, *resting* it, and *exercising* it. Example: right now, I'm exercising a writing ability. I'll soon be resting my body. Tomorrow I'll feed my relationships by meeting someone for lunch.

IDOLIZING THE GOLDEN EGGS

Beware of loving the blessings (golden eggs) more than the source of those blessings (the goose). Do that and you'll eventually lose both.

The farmer grew impatient and greedy. He reduced his pet to a commodity—a thing that gave him things. When he killed the goose, all he had left was his idolatrous heart and a world of regret.

But he sacrificed more than a bird to learn this lesson. He lost his character. Bad enough when it's a farm animal. Tragic when you've lost a career. Or a child. A ministry. A testimony.

THE GOLD IS IN THE GRIND

Most of the fulfilling things in life (golden eggs) happen in the grind. Consistent, non-glamorous, day-in-and-day-out work (feeding the goose) is the gateway to prosperity.

To get the golden eggs, the farmer needed three essential qualities: *patience*, *daily contact* with the goose, and *care* for the goose. That's true in our finances, relationships, and personal lives too. We experience God's blessing through patience, daily disciplines, and constant care. That's rarely exciting or glamorous, but it's necessary.

The key here is consistency. Doing a little work regularly is better than massive efforts done occasionally.

NO SHORTCUTS OR SHORT CIRCUITS

You can't short-circuit God's plan. The Israelites learned that when they tried to horde manna. The farmer learned it when he killed his goose in his haste for eggs. You and I will learn that whenever we try to shortcut or presume upon God.

There's more to waiting than the delay of a long-desired outcome. When you've done all you can do today and must wait until later to do more, that too is waiting. The waiting of incremental progress. The waiting that can't rush the process.

THE GLORY OF THE ORDINARY

Your greatest sources of joy and blessing (golden eggs) come from everyday sources. The most familiar and ordinary factors in your life (your geese) create the most value. That's easy to overlook in the search for something new and exciting.

Look for the gold in familiar places first. That includes family, friends, home, work, and your gifts and talents. Sometimes those factors are so common to us, we don't recognize their power and impact.

GOD'S FRAMEWORK FOR BLESSING

God is neither a goose nor a golden egg dispenser. He is God! But He *has* created a framework to help us experience His benefits and blessings. That framework always involves four crucial ingredients:

1. Faith in Him as our ultimate source

> *Every good action and every perfect gift is from God. These good gifts come down from the Creator of the sun, moon, and stars, who does not change like their shifting shadows.*
>
> James 1:17, NCV

Avoid idolizing either the blessing or the earthly source. God and God alone gives every rich treasure. All your desires, all your ambitions, are ultimately found in Him.

2. Gratitude for the benefits and blessings we have already received

> "'Give thanks to the LORD Almighty,
> for the Lord is good;
> his love endures forever.'
>
> "For I will restore the fortunes of the land as they were before," says the Lord.
>
> Jeremiah 33:11, NIV

There's a direct connection in scripture between gratitude and abundance. Thankfulness recognizes the abundance God has already provided. And it positions us to receive even more from Him.

3. Development of the earthly channels through which He blesses us

> You Philippians well know, and you can be sure I'll never forget it, that when I first left Macedonia province, venturing out with the Message, not one church helped out in the give-and-take of this work except you.
>
> Philippians 4:15, MSG

Paul was a master at this, even in prison. He nurtured relationships that were sources of strength and provision.

Think of who or what God could use in your life. That certainly includes people. But it could also mean your own skills. Your gifts. Sources of knowledge. What can you do to nurture those channels?

Don't wait until you have a major problem. Cultivate relationships, stretch your talent today, and encourage the faith and strength of your sources today.

4. The passage of time

> *Therefore be patient, brethren, until the coming of the Lord. The farmer waits for the precious produce of the soil, being patient about it, until it gets the early and late rains. You too be patient; strengthen your hearts, for the coming of the Lord is near.*
>
> James 5:7–8

Much of the Christian life is lived in the white spaces between the verses. Every blessing has its due season. Sometimes the season feels eternally long. Other times it's lightning-fast.

Regardless of the timing, *the abundance of the blessing is forged in the waiting seasons.* Aesop's farmer didn't get it. LifeVestors do. But as you'll discover in the next section, your confidence will be tested during those seasons.

SEED MONEY

1. "Your geese are the sources God uses to produce value you want. But unlike the fable, you have more than one goose. You have a gaggle of them." List the people or other things that function as potential geese in your life. Then rate your care of those geese on a 1–10 scale, where 10 means great care and 1 means great neglect.

2. "Regardless of the timing, *the abundance of the blessing is forged in the waiting seasons.*" Where and how do you find it hard at times to wait for God's timing?

3. Read Hebrews 10:35–36. What are the characteristics of a believer who waits well?

4. Based on what you read in this section, how will you position yourself to wait with confidence on the Lord to fulfill His promise(s)?

The Ultimate Test
Where Waiting Meets Leadership

We live in a world awash with expectations of push-button success and results. So what do you do when you've done everything and still haven't seen what you *long for* and *expect* to see?

Sometimes . . .

- Like Mr. Holland, you sacrifice your dreams to help others fulfill theirs. But nobody gathers for your final "concert."
- People don't look you up to thank you for the encouragement you gave them.
- People you trust betray that trust. People you love don't love you back. Those you build your hopes on let you down.
- You get out of the boat and wind up wet and cold, with the wrong kind of publicity.
- You do everything you know to finish well, but the results you want still lurk on the horizon.
- You see mercy-drop miracles—down payments on dreams to come. But the ultimate dream eludes you.

Was it all a waste? Were you crazy to believe, stupid to try? Well, you're in good company. Remember those friends in high places?

> *Not one of these people, even though their lives of faith were exemplary, got their hands on what was promised. God had a better plan for us: that their faith and our faith would come together to make one completed whole, their lives of faith not complete apart from ours.*
>
> Hebrews 11:39-40, MSG

There's more to faith, influence, and legacies than results. Especially results in your lifetime. Sometimes others harvest what you've planted, or build on your foundation.

Unfair? It depends on who's keeping score. Abraham and Abel planted, and *will* get their reward. But God in His wisdom wanted *you* and *me* to share it too. Same goes for those who may benefit from your life and influence.

If leading and investing your life were easy, the results would be cheap. But greater returns call for perseverance and gritty faith. And that *will* be tested.

THE REWARD IS IN THE BELIEVING

Sometimes the reward is in the believing itself. It's in the intimacy with God that only comes when He tests your faith and you pass or fail. (Yes, there is intimacy with God, even in your failures.)

For example, would you obey God, even when you're the only one doing so? Noah did (Hebrews 11:7, Genesis 6). There were no Ark Committees, no Ark Community. Just Noah, the kook, who built that crazy contraption, presumably with only the help of his family.

Would you obey God when you had no clue where He's taking you? Abraham did (Hebrews 11:8). All he had was his family, livestock, and a promise from God. No destination. No roots. No security. No home—just a tent. No retirement plan—just the offer of an incredible journey. For Abraham every encounter was a new adventure in believing.

Will you wait for God's timing? Abraham learned that one the hard way. But he learned to trust that God's timing, while hardly ever ours, is always perfect.

Would you believe God, even when His promise is a physical impossibility? Sarah did (Hebrews 11:11). The very idea was crazy! Even she laughed at the mention of a son in her old age. But God can bring life out of death and hope out of despair. He delights in doing the impossible and delights even more in those who believe Him for it.

Would you trust God, even when it means sacrificing that which you cherish most? Abraham did. And the Bible records it in excruciating detail. Abraham faithfully obeyed God's command to surrender the son he'd waited for all his life (Genesis 22).

Would you trust God to the point that you're willing to suffer in order to fulfill God's purpose? Moses did.

> *He thought that it was better to suffer for the promised Christ than to own all the treasures of Egypt.*
>
> Hebrews 11:26, TLB

Would you endure, when the easiest thing to do is quit? Moses did. He endured family separation. Identity crisis. Social rejection. Personal failure. Hostile governments. Life-threatening situations. And a throng of three million crybabies. Through all that, he was called the meekest man on earth (see Numbers 12:3).

Will you trust God, even when you're about to be overwhelmed? Remember what Moses said to the Israelites, when they had their backs to the Red Sea?

> *"Stop being so fearful! Remain steady, and you will see how ADONAI is going to save you. He will do it today—today you have seen the Egyptians, but you will never see them again!"*
>
> Exodus 14:13, CJB

I'll have to admit—the loud words shooting from my mouth in those overwhelming circumstances? Probably not so courageous or believing.

BELIEVING VS. DEMANDING

When you're waiting, there's a difference between believing and demanding. After the death of Lazarus, Mary and Martha both expressed the exact same words to Jesus:

> *"Lord, if You had been here, my brother would not have died."*
>
> John 11:21, 32

One produced a tender argument. The other resulted in Jesus weeping. What was the difference? Martha had a faith that demanded. Mary had a faith that submitted.

What are you believing God for? Healing? Restoration of your marriage? Financial provision? A friend? The salvation or spiritual return of your children? Professional success? Your business to thrive? Read this carefully:

> *God always honors faith, but He doesn't always deliver*
> *the results we expect or demand.*

It's the ultimate test, and I've blown it. Often. *Will you continue to display confidence in God, even when He doesn't deliver, per your instructions?*

CONFESSIONS OF A POUTER

I wish I could be pen pals with whoever wrote the 73rd psalm. We think a lot alike. I title this, "Confessions of a Pouter," because he blew it like I blow it sometimes. But there are wonderful lessons he learned through his experience.

He learned that . . .

Things are not always what they appear to be.

Success in life does not depend on where we are but where we are headed.

Those who trust in themselves are standing in a slippery place.

Most importantly, he learned that *God* is "what's in it for you"! In humble celebration and sheepish discovery, he exclaims,

> *Whom have I in heaven but you?*
> *I desire you more than anything on earth.*
> *My health may fail, and my spirit may grow weak,*
> *but God remains the strength of my heart;*
> *he is mine forever.*
>
> Psalm 73:25–26, NLT

The supreme test of your leadership is not what you did to succeed. It's what—or Whom—you cling to in the wake of your disappointment. As we'll see in the next section, LifeVestors don't give losses the final word.

SEED MONEY

1. "Sometimes others harvest what you've planted, or build on your foundation." What have you inherited that you didn't work for? What do you want future generations to experience because of your work or influence?

2. Based on the tests mentioned in this section, how is your faith being tested right now? How are you responding?

3. Read Psalm 73. How did the "pouting psalmist" change his perspective on his testing season? How can you learn from his example during the times your faith is tested?

4. What action step can you take to demonstrate your faith during your waiting season?

Restoring Your Losses
Where Waiting Meets Increase

I know what you may be thinking. It's easy to talk about results when the playing field is level. Easy to talk about fulfilled promises when we're making progress. But your situation's different, right? You've been punched in the gut. Your dreams turned to disappointments. You experienced a major setback—maybe your fault, maybe another's, maybe nobody's. You found yourself in a hole.

Give God time? For what? More gut punches?

Increase? Ha! The name of your game is survival. Your back's to the wall and your future just flew out the window.

FROM SETBACK TO COMEBACK

Before you can multiply your results, you may first have to restore your losses. If you've had a setback, you need a comeback. The good news is that coming back doesn't depend on your ability or wisdom. But you do have to cooperate with God's restoration process.

Frank Reich knows a little about that. Frank was a backup quarterback for the Buffalo Bills, pressed into a starting role on January 3, 1993. It was the AFC wild card game, and the Bills were hosting the Houston Oilers and legendary quarterback Warren Moon. Winner moves on; loser goes home; it was terrible time for your star starter to go down. The first half was ugly. At halftime Moon's Houston Oilers led the Bills 35–3.

It was one of the greatest comebacks in NFL history.

Sometimes we experience adversity and, like the Bills, face impossible odds. It's "halftime," but we're ready to call it quits. This usually involves loss of some kind. Jay lost his job. Carol lost her son. Alice lost her health—nearly her life. Mike lost his best friend. Chuck lost Peggy, his wife. Larry lost financial security when his business went south. All these are real people who experienced real losses. And the last thing they wanted to talk about was any expectation of increase.

Then there was Job. Went from the pinnacle to the potty. Lost everything but his wife and his life (see Job 1–2). But Job had an amazing ending. After all he went through, the conclusion is almost anticlimactic.

> *"And the LORD restored Job's losses when he prayed for his friends."*
> Job 42:10, NKJV

That verse, simple as it is, gives me great hope. It encourages me that God restored Job's losses.

Who took them away? Satan.

Who brought them back? God.

Did Job deserve it? Not if you read the greatest tongue-lashing in the history of tongue-lashing. That went on for *four chapters* (see Job 38–41). The Lord was done with Job's whining.

And yet God, in His grace, snatched victory from defeat. He restored everything Job had lost, with interest. Yes, this took time. How long? Long enough for Job to have ten more kids (see Job 42:12–13)! (And you wanted it how soon?) God has His timing, but He does reveal progress along the way.

JOB'S JOURNEY BACK

God did the restoring. But He required Job to participate in the process. Job had to fight the fight of faith. He had lost everything near and dear to him. Now he had to believe God again for increase, when all he'd seen for a long time was decrease.

How about you? Do you have enough faith and hope to believe God can give you back "the years that the locusts have eaten" (Joel 2:18–27)? Maybe we can learn a few things from the way Job positioned himself to receive, even after he'd lost so much.

1. Job recognized God as a God of purpose.

> *"I know that You can do everything,*
> *And that no purpose of Yours can be withheld from You."*
>
> Job 42:2, NKJV

Job still had no answers to his questions. But he'd been reminded of God's stubborn determination to fulfill His purpose. Job recognized that God's purposes are good and submitted to them, even when he didn't have answers. He didn't give in to cynicism. He refused to interpret his disappointments as evidence that God was out to get him.

2. Job confessed his whining spirit.

> *"I was talking about things I knew nothing about and did not understand."*
>
> Job 42:3, TLB

Job saw that he'd taken his words too far. Things spoken in pain often reveal our ignorance and pride. Remember, nobody ever solved a problem or changed a situation by whining or demanding. If you want to see your losses restored, quit your bellyaching.

3. Job went from hearing God to seeing Him.

Job's previous relationship with God had served him well. But in his unspeakable pain, he needed more.

> *God will not give you more than you can handle. But He will allow you to face adversity that your previous experience isn't big enough to handle.*

Job went from hearing about God's voice to seeing God's face. From serving God by reputation to serving God by revelation. He told the Lord, "I had heard about you before, but now I have seen you" (Job 42:5, TLB).

When life gets desperate, it isn't enough to hear stories about God. You need to lay hold of God until He shows up. Just remember, when God does show up, like Job you may get more than you bargained for.

4. Job confronted his ugly side.

Adversity often reveals a side of ourselves that on our better days we don't like. That was true of Job. He found a part of himself he hated. And there he repented before God.

> *"Therefore I despise myself and repent in dust and ashes."*
> Job 42:6, NIV

I love this. Here was a man God favored, still recognizing his need to get his act together. Whenever I go through adversity I always see something in myself that I'm ashamed of—even if others don't see it. In fact, the whole point of testing is to reveal to us the flaws in our character.

5. Job prayed for his friends.

This is significant for several reasons. First, he was praying for people who had failed him at his greatest point of need. Second, he was obeying God and showing mercy and forgiveness to men who had sinned against him. Third, he refused to gloat over being right.

How about you? Have you been disappointed? Have you known people who kicked you when you were down? Or knocked you down in the first place? Pray for them. Pray that God would help them. Bless them. Draw them to Himself. Reveal Himself to them. It will transform you as much or more as it does them.

You may be down for the count, and the last thing you feel like doing is investing your life in something or someone. It's time for a counterattack.

Quit whining.

Start recognizing and celebrating God as a God of purpose.

Take a hard look at yourself, but don't stop looking until you've "looked" at the Lord.

Oh, and one more thing. Let the devil know that every time he throws something at you, you're going to pray for one of your friends . . . or one of his.

Frank Reich got it. The comeback quarterback who made history on January 3, 1993, met the press after that famous game. There he gave the words to Shawn Craig's song as his testimony:

> *In Christ alone I place my trust,*
> *And find my glory in the power of the cross*
> *In every victory, let it be said of me*
> *My source of strength,*
> *My source of hope is Christ alone.*[1]

It's time to expect that increase. Just remember Who restores your losses.

SEED MONEY

1. Read 2 Corinthians 4:7–18. What battles was Paul facing, and what characterized his response?

2. "God will not give you more than you can handle. But He *will* allow you to face adversity that your previous experience isn't big enough to handle." How have you faced hardship that was beyond your previous experience? How did you respond? What did God teach you in the process?

3. Is it time for a counterattack? Do you feel like you've been pushed around by the devil or your circumstances? Form a counterattack plan, based on the five things that Job did.

4. Based on what you've read, what is the first step you can take to restore losses that you may have experienced?

Trouble in the Waiting Room
Where Waiting Meets Freedom

How do you handle the fact that God has promised to meet all your needs (see Philippians 4:19), yet you have an unmet need?

How do you respond when God promises to give you your heart's desires (see Psalm 37:4), yet you have unfulfilled desires?

What do you say to a single person who longs to be married? A wife who's lonely in her marriage? A couple that tries to honor God with their finances, yet the only result is more pressure? A student who feels called into ministry and longs to be there, but keeps having doors slammed in his face?

These are examples of waiting seasons—living with unfulfilled desires, unfulfilled promises, and unmet needs. They're the stuff of maturity. The cold chisel that, with the blows of God's hammer, knocks off pieces of you that don't look like Jesus.

Waiting seasons are a staple of biblical life stories. Sarah and Abraham wanted a son (see Genesis 15:1–4). Wait.

Hannah wanted one too (see 1 Samuel 1:1–11). You know the drill.

Jacob, smitten by his love for Rachel, worked for seven years to win her hand in marriage. "But they seemed like only a few days to him because of his love for her" (Genesis 29:20, NIV). Tricked by his father-in-law into another seven years, it wasn't quite so romantic.

David wanted to build a temple in Jerusalem. God said wait (see 2 Samuel 7).

Paul begged the Lord three times to get rid of that "messenger of Satan," that thorn in his flesh. God's answer: "My grace is sufficient for you" (2 Corinthians 12:9). Translation: not anytime soon.

Nothing can set you up for high-octane growth like being in a waiting season. But that can also expose you to major failure.

This section explores the potential glory and trouble of life in the waiting room. You'll also find some practical suggestions for finding freedom there.

A REASON FOR ALL THIS

Psalm 37 is written to believers who've just been deposited into the holding cell. In this heartfelt song, David, now a seasoned and wise man, encourages young sons and daughters in the faith. With a reassuring voice and warm heart, he says, "Relax. The end of the story has yet to be told. God has a plan and a purpose."

The Lord uses waiting seasons to increase our confidence in Him. He wants to strengthen our ability to "commit everything you do to the LORD" (Psalm 37:5, NLT).

Sometimes God is fulfilling His own timing. He's giving the wicked one more shot before it's curtains.

Occasionally the waiting room reveals the rage or some other sin that's just beneath your veneer.

God also wants to build meekness in you—the quality of bearing "strength under control."

He uses the waiting room to deepen your perspective. There He unpacks a measure of wisdom in you that you couldn't receive any other way.

And finally, God uses the waiting to finish off a season of obedience.

A DANGER IN ALL THIS TOO

Read about somebody else's waiting season and it sure can seem easy. Maybe touched by a minor weakness here or there, but otherwise it's a stroll down Character Building Lane. Read David's advice, however, and you get a different picture. I wonder how he knew all that?

> Don't worry about the wicked
>> or envy those who do wrong.
> For like grass, they soon fade away.
>> Like springtime flowers, they soon wither.
> Trust in the LORD and do good.
>> Then you will live safely in the land and prosper.
> Take delight in the LORD,
>> and he will give you your heart's desires.
> Commit everything you do to the LORD.
>> Trust him, and he will help you.
> He will make your innocence radiate like the dawn,
>> and the justice of your cause will shine like the noonday sun.
> Be still in the presence of the LORD,
>> and wait patiently for him to act.
> Don't worry about evil people who prosper
>> or fret about their wicked schemes.
> Stop being angry!
>> Turn from your rage!
> Do not lose your temper—
>> it only leads to harm.
>
> Psalm 37:1–8, NLT

Nobody wants to admit they're jealous. But go through a season where undeserving people appear to be prospering and you aren't! I've lost count of the number of times I said or wrote, "God is doing it for everybody else. Why won't He do it for me?"

The short answer is, He won't do it for me because I'm so stinking jealous of everything He does for everybody else.

Disobedience is another threat during the waiting season. Keep doing the next right thing, David counsels. Don't shortcut or back up on your obedience to

God. Otherwise, you may find yourself repeating the same class.

Idolatry can be a problem. When you delight in the desires of *your* heart rather than in the Lord, you're cutting yourself off from both.

Impatience? Could that possibly surface during a waiting season? Whining impatience? Angry impatience? "Let's help God out" impatience?

Then there's bitterness. By the time Eli gave Hannah the good news, she looked more drunk than desperate. She'd worn the pain of waiting so long, it even cut her off from the love of her husband (see 1 Samuel 1).

MEANWHILE, BACK ON THE FARM

One of the problems we have with waiting is that we don't know how. We think of waiting as the kind of thing you do in a doctor's office. James offers a different idea:

> *The farmer waits for the precious produce of the soil, being patient about it, until it gets the early and late rains. You too be patient; strengthen your hearts.*
>
> James 5:7–8

Waiting on God is anything but idle. The farmers I know spend about two weeks out of the year harvesting. What are they doing the rest of the time?

Clearly defining what the harvest is.

Creating an environment where the life in the seed can be nurtured. That means plowing, fertilizing, irrigating, or even improving the seed.

Then sowing faithfully. Weeding carefully. Removing obstacles to fruitfulness without damaging the harvest itself.

Then maintaining—taking care of equipment and other types of administration.

> *Their harvest is determined by what they do while they're waiting.*

How does that apply to us when we're in the waiting seasons? Try this series of questions to help you think through those times in your life:

1. What is my harvest? What result am I waiting for?

2. Is today a harvest day? If yes, then enjoy the results. Deliver your professional service, attend the event, collect the money, whatever. If not, then . . .

3. What can I do to cultivate? How can I prepare my mental, spiritual, or emotional strength for my harvest?

4. How can I plant a seed to move toward my harvest? In the natural, this is a marketing or initiative question. Sowing may mean making a phone call. Or following up a previous conversation. In the spiritual, this is a question of prayer and obedience to the Spirit's promptings. You're asking, "Lord, what's my assignment for today?"

5. What potential threats do I see to the harvest, and how can I address them today? This may mean dealing with conflicts or encouraging yourself. It may mean spiritual warfare or intercessory prayer.

6. What administrative things do I need to do during this waiting period? What details can I work on so that when my harvest arrives I'll be ready?

"Strengthen your heart," James says. That's what waiting is for. You'll never see freedom without it. But as you'll see in the next section, not all waiting is a grind. Sometimes it's downright fun.

SEED MONEY

1. Read through Psalm 37 and make a list of the promises the Lord makes to His people.

2. "[Waiting seasons are] the stuff of maturity. The cold chisel that, with the blows of God's hammer, knocks off pieces of you that don't look like Jesus." How has God matured you through seasons of waiting? How does what He has done in the past speak to your current circumstances?

3. Read Psalm 37:1–11. What specific, positive actions does David recommend? How easy or hard are these for you right now, and why?

4. Choose a goal or dream you are waiting for. Go through the six questions above and create an action plan for moving forward.

How to Get Your A-Game Back

When Waiting Meets Eternity

Got caught several years ago. I'm talking deer-in-the-headlights, flat-footed, let-me-know-if-I'm-drooling caught. All with a simple question.

"What are you looking forward to right now?" he asked.

Huh?

Say that again?

What are you looking forward to?

Cue the crickets.

I was coming off two weeks of intense work, up until about 2:00 a.m. every night. I was in head-down, just-get-it-done mode. Who has time to think ahead?

Precisely.

I had no clue how to answer that because I wasn't looking forward to anything.

Enough about me. How about you? What are you looking forward to?

I took some time to think more about that question over the next several days. Especially after Cassie, my daughter, arrived that same night with her vintage Mickey Mouse planning notebook. The whole family was planning a Christmas trip to Disney. Now there she sat—*four months in advance*—already living the trip. She'd picked out the restaurants where we would dine. She had detailed maps of the whole Magic domain. She logged onto websites offering advice for avoiding the long lines.

In short, Cassie showed up with her A-game—her *anticipation* game. And she inspired me to find my own.

In a chapter on waiting, we've spent a lot of time discussing how hard it can be. The stuff of endurance and perseverance. But waiting has another tale to tell. The story of anticipation—knowing that in due season we'll experience that desired vision.

Here's the bottom line on anticipation: You can't look forward when you spend too much time looking back. Or with your head down, getting stuff done.

You can't look forward when you dread the future or lack expectancy.

You can't look forward if "forward" looks like the same-old, same-old and you're bored.

So if that describes you, as it described me, here are a few places to come up for air and restore the joy of anticipation.

SPIRITUAL

You get your A-game back by reconnecting with the One who holds the future in the first place. He's *full* of anticipation. Check this out:

> *"Eye has not seen, nor ear heard,*
> *Nor have entered into the heart of man*
> *The things which God has prepared for those who love Him."*
>
> 1 Corinthians 2:9, NKJV

What if some of those things weren't limited to the time after you die? What if just one of those things awaited you tomorrow? *What if the only way you could discover it was to be expecting it?*

MENTAL

You get your A-game back by thinking about the possibilities, not just the realities. In other words, LifeVestor, take time to envision, to dream. One of my favorite Bible verses has to do with travel plans:

> *For a great and effective door has opened to me, and there are many adversaries.*
>
> 1 Corinthians 16:9, NKJV

Paul had a choice—look at the open door or dwell on the adversaries. You have the same choice. And your attitude will follow your focus.

EMOTIONAL

You get your A-game back by rising above current stress and past sorrows. You do that by reconnecting with what and whom you love.

Who do you know who seems to make the time fly by when you're with them? What do you love to do that you get so lost in it you could enjoy it for hours? Maybe it's time to refill your emotional tank—especially if you've been running on fumes for a while.

VOLITIONAL

You get your A-game back by choosing to. It's a matter of faith and will. If your life is nothing more than grinding it out or dreading what comes next, you have no one to blame but yourself. You may not be able to choose the actions or attitudes of others, but you do have control of your own. You can't control your circumstances, but you can control your attitude toward them.

On my keyboard I can make one single adjustment and go from "SOS" to "wow." I can do the same thing with my attitudes, and so can you.

SELF-ESTEEM

You get your A-game back when you decide you're worthy of a desirable future. Many people lose their A-game when they decide that anticipation is for valuable people. Successful people. Smart people. Popular people. Any people but them.

Careful. Don't make me get all theological on you. Don't make me remind you that the cross of Jesus is an eternal declaration of your worth to God.

Oh, wait. I just did.

FINANCIAL

You get your A-game back when you invest in your future, and don't spend it all today. Save some of your money, but save with a purpose and preferably a timeline. Also try giving your money to the kingdom of God, your church, and worthy causes.

PROFESSIONAL

You get your A-game back when you start crafting a future for your profession. Then invest your time in whatever it takes to make it happen. Yes, I'm talking about vision. A profession without a vision is just a job. And that can serve you fine for the short run. But at some point, what you call a job needs to lift your eyes to the horizons a bit. If your boss or workplace can't do that for you, find one that can, when you can.

FAMILIAL

You get your A-game back when you start enjoying your family today and planning some fun for tomorrow. Even if your nest is empty or your parents are gone. Even if *family* is a painful word for you, there are ways to create some anticipation there. We serve a God who is described as "a father to the fatherless, a defender of widows . . . God sets the lonely in families" (Psalm 68:5-6, NIV). How does it feel to know that He has plans for your loneliness?

INTERPERSONAL

You get your A-game back when you connect with people based on your future, not just your present or past. That's why courtships are so dripping with anticipation. They're in such a discovery mode. It's also why friends who anticipate together and dream together often remain friends for a lifetime.

Who knows you so well that they can point you to your future or restore your sense of hope? Connect with them regularly.

COMMUNAL

You get your A-game back when you engage with a community of people with a vision toward the future. If you don't have any anticipation of your own, you can always borrow some of theirs. And that's why being part of a larger community is important.

ADVERSARIAL

You get your A-game back when you confront the thief who stole it from you in the first place. The enemy comes to steal, kill, and destroy, and one of the first things he takes is our sense of hope or anticipation. It's time to tell the devil to take a hike and give back what he stole from you.

Life isn't all about anticipating the future—it certainly involves living today. But if today is an entree you're enjoying, anticipation is the appetizer and/or the dessert. Aren't you ready for something different? Something sweeter?

What are *you* looking forward to?

SEED MONEY

1. Recall an experience you had as a child in the weeks leading up to Christmas or a birthday. How did you think and act? What did you do while you waited?

2. "You may not be able to choose the actions or attitudes of others, but you do have control of your own. You can't control your circumstances, but you can control your attitude toward them." Take a hard look at your recent attitudes. Better still, ask someone you trust to describe how you come across. How would you or they describe your attitudes?

3. Read Psalm 42. How did David change his attitude from desperation to anticipation?

4. What specific action steps can you take to improve your A-game?

FINAL THOUGHT

Remember Will, the evangelist who took his boys on the scenic route? Their journey of anticipation started with a disappointment. It appeared he hadn't kept his promise. That happens sometimes in our relationship with God as well.

The biggest surprise about the scenic route is
what God will use to get you to your destination.

He'll use disappointments and delays. Difficult people and desperate circumstances. Failure and futility. He'll even use the evil intentions of others. God will take you where you're going. But sometimes He starts you somewhere else to get there.

You'll be tempted to quit. Get angry with God. Give up. Get stupid.

Even more dangerous—you'll be tempted to stop at the candy counter when He has a greater prize waiting.

I have a suggestion. Why not just keep following Him and find joy in the journey? Listen for His voice. Trust His heart. He really does know what He's doing.

After all, if God has you on the scenic route, maybe there's something He actually wants you to *see*.

That Breathless Pause

The white space between the verses. The climax of the movie, complete with a tense musical score, just before the plot is resolved. The silent sky that follows streaks of lightning just before the booming crash of thunder. The bated breath that awaits the first cry of a newborn baby. That small break of silence just before . . . That dramatic, breathless pause.

In life, the breathless pause often lasts only a matter of seconds and is hardly ever discussed. But we've all read about it. And chances are, we've lived it on some level. It's that split-second gap between motion and miracle. When the world for a second or two goes quiet and you're holding your breath with expectancy.

That breathless pause, where you're waiting, anticipating something amazing. When all you have imagined, prayed for, saved for, worked on, and waited for comes to a point of resolution.

THE BIBLE AND THE BREATHLESS PAUSE

The breathless pause shows up with the Israelites between the devil and the deep blue sea. "Don't be afraid!" Moses said. "Stand still and see the salvation of the Lord." So still they stood. And the rest is a history of increase.

But that Red Sea moment didn't start then. It began in the misplaced passion of a young Israelite. The desert wandering of a forgotten shepherd. The call from a burning bush. The courage to return, this time to execute God's plan after forty years of waiting.

You find the breathless pause as a smooth stone rifles from a young shepherd's slingshot toward a giant's fat head.

But the giant slaying didn't start there. It began with a prophet's search for a man after God's own heart. A shepherd boy left to tend sheep while his brothers went off to war. A confrontation with a lion and a bear that turned a songwriter into a warrior and leader.

You find the breathless pause as a guilty king checks on the results of his dastardly decisions for self-glory. Not once, but twice! In one case the king found a fourth man walking in the fiery furnace. In the other, a different king found the lions snoozing in Daniel's den. Both times they found servants of God who were bound by men but free in God's plan.

But royal embarrassment didn't start there. It began with four young men who imagined lives of influence and excellence. Passion to live by God's standards, regardless of their popularity. Execution of daily disciplines, even at the risk of death.

You find the breathless pause as Peter steps out of a boat in a storm and walks toward Jesus. We may never understand his reasons. We may not envy his results. But we all admire his courage and passion.

But the wave walking didn't start there. It started with a professional fisherman, mending his nets, who responded to a higher call. A business miracle that turned into a different mission. An open heart, willing to leave it all on the field (or in the water) to become a fisher of men and pursue a life of abundance.

You find the breathless pause in the seconds after a grave is opened and its chief resident ordered out. "Lazarus come forth!" said the Resurrection and Life.

But the grave robbing didn't start there. It started with three siblings who enjoyed a friendship with Jesus. A home allocated to be His refuge. A discipline of serving and sitting at His feet. A willingness to wait and have their faith stretched in the process.

You find the breathless pause when Peter looks at a lame beggar and imagines him walking. "Silver and gold I do not have, but what I do have I give you: In the name of Jesus Christ of Nazareth, rise up and walk" (Acts 3:6, NKJV).

But healing didn't start there. It started with a risen Christ, casting a world-wide vision for His followers. A ten-day season of waiting and prayer. A transformation of Peter's character. An increase of his capacity.

IN THE MEANTIME

But not every breathless pause happens in an instant. And that could be a problem if you're expecting immediate results. The same Moses who crossed the sea on dry land, after a forty-year sabbatical from Egypt, spent the next forty years in a desert. He died with the Promised Land in his eyes but not under his feet.

The same David who dropped a giant in seconds had to wait years to be king. Despite his anointing by Samuel. God was enlarging his capacity. And more than once he hollered, "How long, O Lord?"

The same Daniel who snoozed with the lions had to endure three or four different pagan kings. Add to that a host of jealous peers and a lifetime of spiritually grinding it out day after day in captivity.

The same Peter who took center stage at Pentecost saw the church in Jerusalem scattered to the winds. He also watched his own leadership take second fiddle to Paul's.

The same Lazarus who emerged from his own grave eventually got sick and died again. Ditto for those disciples who witnessed the resurrection and ascension of Jesus. They waited every day for His return, only to die never seeing it.

The point: if you're living in that breathless pause and the next day you're still holding your breath, it's OK to exhale. Just because you aren't seeing your miracle, your dream, your next step happen instantly doesn't mean the Lord is uninterested or unable.

Delays are not rejections.

Disappointments are not defeats.

Be ready for God's next "suddenly." The breathless pause will end. The investment you make with your life could produce a return when and in ways you least expect it. But while you're waiting, train for the long haul and the "meantime." God is just as involved in your suffocating waiting as He is in your breathless pause. And it's no less miraculous if it takes nine months or ninety years than if the deed is done in seconds.

Keep dreaming, my LifeVesting friend. Keep caring deeply. Focus. Execute. Grow. Wait. Then breathe. Exhale. Trust. Believe. Suddenly or not, the miracle is coming.

In due season you *will* reap if you just don't quit.

Notes

CHAPTER 2

1. Jerrold Mundis. *How to Get out of Debt, Stay out of Debt, and Live Prosperously: Based on the Proven Principles and Techniques of Debtors Anonymous,* rev. ed. (New York: Bantam, 2012).

CHAPTER 6

1. Randy Stonehill, "Puppet Strings," track 5 on *Welcome to Paradise* (Solid Rock Records, 1976, vinyl. Used by permission.
2. Oswald Chambers, *My Utmost for His Highest* (New York: Dodd, Mead & Co., 1935), November 1.

CHAPTER 8

1. Andrew Shawn Craig and Don Koch (music and lyrics), "In Christ Alone," New Spring Publishing, Inc., 1994. Used by permission.

About the Author

Andy Wood has been on his own LifeVesting journey for a long time. As a pastor, speaker, author, professor, and executive coach, he has devoted his life to one simple idea: MADISEL – an acronym for "make a difference in some else's life!" That's what has driven him for the last 40 years as he has invested his life in communicating truth with passion and personally coaching, challenging, and encouraging others. He has a Ph.D. in Organizational Leadership, 32 years of church and nonprofit leadership experience, and 18 years' experience as a university professor, where he has taught more than 10,000 future leaders. Andy lives on his family farm in southwest Alabama with Robin, his wife of 38 years.

Take Your LifeVesting Journey Deeper!

ife Vesting is more than information – it is aimed at transformation. If you're ready to experience even greater growth, passion, freedom, and impact, check out these resources:

- The *LifeVesting* live experience. This six-hour live event is coming to a location near you. OR you may be interested in hosting a live experience in a seminar, workshop, or retreat setting. Here Andy and his team will share with you in person how you can jump-start a journey of abundance, leadership, increase, freedom, and eternal significance.

- *LifeVesting* coaching groups. Join 8-12 others who, with Andy or a trained coach, will take you on an eight-week journey of mutual growth and encouragement. These groups are offered either virtually or in person throughout the year and include one individual coaching session.

- *LifeVesting* one-day intensives. Immerse yourself or your team in a 6-8 hour personalized coaching and consulting experience, applying what you have learned to your life, family, career, leadership, ministry, and/ or organization. These experiences are individually crafted for maximum impact based on your unique needs and goals. They include three one-hour follow-up coaching sessions.

- *LifeVesting* individual coaching. A 10-week coaching journey that guides you through the process of writing your own LifeVesting story and crafting your own LifeVesting plan.

- *LifeVesting* coach and facilitator training. Imagine being able to help others by becoming a certified *LifeVesting* coach and facilitator. You will get personalized training from Andy, access to all materials at wholesale or cost, and support. A great resource for coaches, pastors, teachers, and counselors.

- The *LifeVesting* 40-week personal intensive. This experience takes you on a deep dive, working personally with Andy, to envision, execute, and protect your own unique LifeVesting plan. In addition to the personal coaching, you will also have unlimited access to live events, a coaching group, and coach/facilitator training at no additional charge.

Check out our website – http://lifevesting.com for more information on each of these options and a schedule of live events.

A free ebook edition is available with the purchase of this book.

To claim your free ebook edition:

1. Visit MorganJamesBOGO.com
2. Sign your name CLEARLY in the space
3. Complete the form and submit a photo of the entire copyright page
4. You or your friend can download the ebook to your preferred device

Print & Digital Together Forever.

Snap a photo

Free ebook

Read anywhere

CPSIA information can be obtained
at www.ICGtesting.com
Printed in the USA
JSHW030341111221
21201JS00001B/32